D1374375

CASSELL'S PET AND FANCY BOOKS

BEES AND BEEKEEPING

by A. V. Pavord

CASSELL · LONDON

CASSELL & COMPANY LTD

an imprint of
Cassell & Collier Macmillan Publishers Ltd
35 Red Lion Square, London WC1R 4SG
and at Sydney, Auckland, Toronto, Johannesburg

and an affiliate of The Macmillan Company Inc, New York

First published 1970
Second edition 1975

I.S.B.N. 0 304 93632 4

Printed in Great Britain by
REDWOOD BURN LIMITED
Trowbridge & Esher

CONTENTS

ACKNOWLEDGEMENTS FOR PHOTOGRAPHS

Stephen Dalton (Natural History Photographic Agency), cover picture, frontispiece and photographs 2 and 4.

G. H. Hewison, Bee Research Association Picture Library, photographs 1, 3, and 5.

By courtesy of P. S. Milne, National Agricultural Advisory Service, photographs 6 to 11.

By courtesy of Rothamsted Experimental Station (Copyright reserved), photographs 12, 13, 14, 16 and 17.

By permission of the Controller of Her Majesty's Stationery Office (Crown Copyright), photographs 15 and 18.

Introduction

Honeybees have always fascinated men. Their complex, mysterious system of life, their instinctive yet highly organized production of honey and their language — a language of dances — second only to our own are for bee-keepers an endless source of interest and for scientists an astounding subject for research. So much is known about these small insects; so much more is still to be discovered.

Throughout the world wherever conditions are favourable honeybees may be found; and beekeepers have not been slow to follow their example. Beekeeping is an absorbing and relaxing hobby that appeals to people of all walks of life and of all nationalities. It can be enjoyed as a lifetime occupation or as a weekend hobby, since unlike other kinds of livestock honeybees can look after themselves and do not require regular attention from their owners.

Even with a minimum of attention beekeeping is a profitable hobby: with modern methods, all of which are fully described in this book, a strong, well-housed colony of honeybees will provide for their keeper's use some twenty-five to thirty pounds of honey a season; in good summers there may be three times as much.

At honey shows, held annually by most county and local beekeeping associations (see Appendix), beekeepers are able to exhibit their produce and to exchange hints and ideas with their competitors. The hobby is well served by magazines and other publications: *Bee Craft* is published monthly and *Bee World* quarterly, while advisory leaflets from the Ministry of Agriculture, Fisheries and Food can be obtained for the price of a stamped, addressed envelope.

In schools beekeeping is often the basis of a group or club activity, providing countless interesting avenues of study. No other form of livestock has had a longer history nor offers such a convenient, wide and varied scope for centres of inter-est ranging through biology, woodwork, mathematics, geography and cookery — and the bees look after themselves

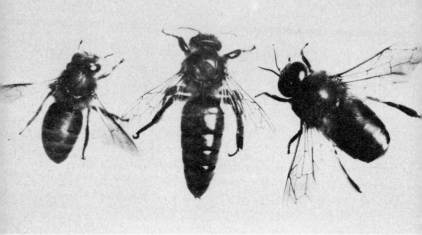

Photograph 1 The honeybee: worker, queen, drone.

at weekends, during school holidays and throughout the winter.

Most beekeepers have only two to four colonies of bees, but in good areas a few keep bees on a scale large enough to give them a livelihood. Together they make a considerable contribution to the nation's food supply both in the form of marketed honey and in the increased quality and quantity of the fruit and seed crops pollinated, as a free service, by their bees.

CHAPTER 1
Bee Life and the Beekeeper

The antiquity of honeybees is greater than that of man. Honeybees existed as social insects living and working in well-organized communities long before man appeared on earth. Evolution has established a close association between flowers and honeybees. The bees, in search of essential food-stuffs, gather pollen and nectar from flowers and in so doing effect the pollination necessary for the setting of seed. Nectar, the carbohydrate energy-producing food, is elaborated by the bees into honey which will keep for long periods. The pollen, the protein body-building food, is used in the feeding of bee larvae.

Beespace and Movable Combs. In 1851 an American, L. L. Langstroth, by careful observation and trials found out that honeybees would leave a clear beeway (or 'beespace') between and around the combs in the hive. He made rect-angular frames of wood within which the bees were en-couraged to build their combs. These frames were separated from the hive walls by a gap exactly the width of a natural beespace ($\frac{1}{4}$ to $\frac{5}{16}$ in.). Bees respected this gap and did not fill it up with beeswax or propolis. The framed combs, hanging freely, could be easily moved, examined and manipulated. This important discovery led to the invention of many types of hives and other beekeeping appliances such as excluders and honey-extractors. Now we have the movable-comb hive which not only simplifies beekeeping practice but has made possible those observations of bee life, behaviour and colony life which a successful beekeeper needs to understand in order to work with the bees.

The Honeybee Colony. In the hive the honeybee colony is composed of worker bees, a queen (the mother of the colony) and drones (male bees), as on page 2. In the spring and summer the colony also contains eggs, laid by the queen in the hexagonal cells of the honeycomb, which hatch into larvae, change into pupae and emerge from the cells as young

3

bees. The eggs, bee larvae and pupae are usually collectively called the 'brood'.

At the peak of its strength in the summer a good, healthy, normal colony of honeybees will consist of the queen, perhaps as many as fifty thousand workers, a few hundred drones and the combs containing developing brood and stores of honey and pollen.

FROM EGG TO BEE

The honeybee undergoes a complete metamorphosis, or sequence of changes, in its four stages (egg, larva, pupa and adult insect). The duration of each stage varies with the caste (queen, worker, or drone), as shown in Table 1.

The queen bee can lay two types of egg. One kind which produces female bees (workers or queens) is impregnated with male sperm from the spermatheca (sperm sac) as it passes down the oviduct from the ovaries (see page 8). The other kind does not receive the male sperm and can only develop into drones. Thus female bees inherit characteristics

Table 1. AVERAGE DEVELOPMENT TIMES (DAYS) OF HONEYBEES

	QUEEN	WORKER	DRONE
Incubation of the Egg	3	3	3
Feeding the Larva	5	5	6
Spinning a Cocoon	1	2	3
Period of Rest	2	3	4
Change from Larva to Pupa	1	1	1
Pupa or Nymph	3	7	7
Emergence of Adult Bee Total	15	21	24

Queen cells are capped on the 8th or 9th day, worker on the 9th and drone on the 10th.

The above is an average based on normal feeding and broodnest temperatures. Lower temperatures can prolong development times. During the period from spinning the cocoon to the emergence of the bee there is a sequence of continuing progressive changes called metamorphosis.

from both the queen mother and her drone mate, while drones have only those from the queen mother. In the darkness of the hive how does a queen bee know which type of egg, fertilized or unfertilized, to lay in a cell? Very recent research shows that before laying an egg the queen inspects each cell and, by placing her front legs into the cell, is in some way able to assess if sperm is to be withheld when the cell is of the larger (drone) size.

When a female egg is laid by the queen in a worker cell (Diagram 1b) in the broodcomb, it stands upright in relation to the base of the cell. On the second day it leans over and on the third day it lies along the bottom of the cell. Nurse bees now surround it with a small drop of 'bee milk' and the tiny larva emerges from its egg. The larva is now fed for nearly three days on a rich food produced by the nurse bees and for another three days on a 'weaning' mixture of honey (or nectar) and pollen. This feeding by nurse bees is progressive, somewhat meagre in quality and not abundant in quantity. Larval growth is very rapid and the larva casts its skin five times in all to allow for the immense and rapid increase in size and weight. On the ninth day the cell containing the fully grown larva is capped (sealed over) by house bees. Inside, the larva spins a cocoon, develops into a pupa and undergoes metamorphosis. Finally, twenty-one days after the egg was laid, the young adult bee bites her way out of the cell capping and commences her life in the colony.

The eggs destined to become drones are laid in the larger 'drone' cells (Diagram 1a) in the broodcombs. The feeding follows much the same course as with the worker larva, but the pupation stages take three days longer.

Workers and drones are reared in the hexagonal cells which make up the combs in the broodnest but the future queens are reared in acorn-shaped cells built out from the face of the comb (Diagram 1a). These 'queen cells' are usually 1 to $1\frac{3}{8}$ in. long, and taper slightly to an opening at the bottom. The queen cell usually starts as a small waxen cup, about $\frac{3}{8}$ in. across, made by worker bees. In this a female-producing egg is laid. When the small larva emerges after three

5

KINDS OF CELLS

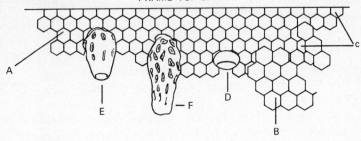

A. Worker Cells — 5 to one inch. B. Drone Cells — 4 to one inch.

C. Transition and Attachment Cells.

D. Queen Cell Cup. E. Open Queen Cell. F. Sealed Queen Cell.

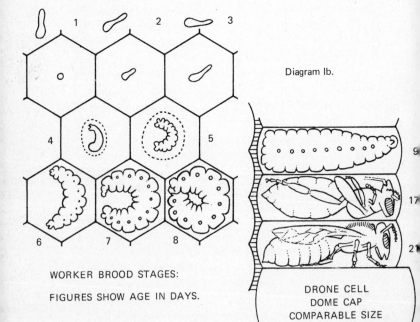

Diagram lb.

WORKER BROOD STAGES:

FIGURES SHOW AGE IN DAYS.

DRONE CELL
DOME CAP
COMPARABLE SIZE

days it is fed lavishly for the next five days on the very rich food 'royal jelly', made by the worker bees, who also enlarge the cell to accommodate the rapidly growing larva. A generous supply of this special food is deposited in the queen cell before it is sealed over on the ninth day and the larva continues feeding for a day or two. Then, in the next seven days, the marvellous changes take place before the perfect young virgin queen emerges, often leaving some unused food at the base of the queen cell.

The fact that a very young female larva can be made into a worker or a queen according to the type of cell used and the very different nutritional food fed during the larval stage is a vital survival factor in bee life. If a colony loses its queen but still has worker eggs or young larvae in the cells, it is able to make another replacement queen. In such an emergency, worker bees can alter the shape and size of the cell in which the young worker larva lies, feed it continuously with 'royal jelly' and so make a queen. Knowledge of this enables bee-keepers to devise methods of rearing queens for replacement and improvement of the strain of bee.

The Queen is the most important of all the hive-dwellers. The attendant workers feed her, groom her and keep her clean. Her duty is to lay eggs, and if she becomes old and/or failing in ability, they arrange for her supersedure. Her body is longer and larger than that of a worker and her abdomen is tapered. Her sting is curved, without barbs and only used against other queens. She has no pollen baskets on her hind legs and no wax-making pockets on the underside of her abdomen. Her wings are short and normally she only flies when on her mating flights or when accompanying the swarm. Other parts of her body are also modified — her head, mouth parts, and internal glands have all undergone changes which further differentiate her from a worker bee.

From an egg genetically exactly the same as those that made her sister worker bees, the queen's whole physiological make-up has been altered by the differential feeding and treatment she received in the larval stages of her life.

The queen has specially well-developed ovaries and an

7

internal organ (the spermatheca) in which the male sperm from the drones at matings is kept alive for several years. It was once thought that the young queen on her mating flight mated with a single drone. Research has now firmly established that it is usual for her to mate several times within a few days before starting to lay eggs. Once egg-laying commences she does not mate again. In good weather conditions, matings are usually effected during the second week of the young queen's life. If unmated after about four weeks, she becomes incapable of mating and can then only lay unfertilized drone eggs.

The queen may live for three or four years — or as long as she is able to lay sufficient viable worker eggs to maintain a strong colony. In beekeeping practice it is best not to retain her in a honey-producing unit for more than two full 'laying' seasons.

The number of workers in the hive depends upon the egg-laying rate of the queen. This, in turn, depends upon the amount of food that she is given by the attendant workers. In the warmer weather of early spring, stimulated by the fresh supplies of pollen and nectar coming into the hive, the queen may start laying a few hundred eggs each day. This rate rapidly increases until in early summer she may be laying as many as 1,800 to 2,000 per day.

Recent research has also shown the importance of one of the queen's specialized glands, the mandibular, which is situated behind her jaws and secretes a complex substance, generally termed *queen substance*. This secretion, as it exudes, is collected by the attendant workers and, distributed by means of food-sharing between them and all other workers, is an important method of communication and colony control. Queen substance is a most important factor in the welding of the workers together as a social unit. Distributed throughout the colony this queen substance has an inhibiting effect on the development of the immature ovaries in worker bees and so prevents 'laying workers'. It also inhibits the formation of queen cells: this effect could well be an important factor in swarm control. Its odour may be part

8

Photograph 2 A court of worker bees attending the queen.

of the colony odour used as a 'password' among bees of the same colony and certainly its scent attracts drones trailing after a young queen on her mating flights. It is also attractive to workers clustering in a swarm. Lack of queen substance (when a queen is old and failing or when she is removed from a colony) is followed by symptoms of queenlessness among the workers, by the formation of emergency queen cells or, if this is not possible, by the appearance of laying workers (see chapter 7).

The worker bees do all the work of the colony. They start work soon after they have emerged from the cell as adult bees, and their life span varies with the amount of work they do. In summer they may work themselves to death in five or six weeks but in autumn and winter they may live for six months. Their work depends chiefly upon their state of physiological development as they age. One of their first duties, after feeding themselves, is to clean out the cells in

9

which the queen will lay eggs. Inside the hive they then feed the older larvae with a mixture of honey and pollen. During this period the brood-food (or 'pharyngeal') glands develop and the youngest larvae and the queen are fed on the special secretion produced (bee milk). When about twelve days old the wax glands on the underside of the worker's abdomen become active and begin to secrete the wax used for comb building. Other glands secrete the enzyme (invertase) which changes the sugars in nectar into honey. Later the development of the sting glands enables the worker bee to become an entrance guard. Some workers will be engaged in fanning with their wings to ventilate the hive; others will receive incoming food supplies and process and store these in the store combs. Evolution and natural selection has fashioned the external and internal body of the worker bee so that all necessary tasks can be efficiently performed.

During the last week or ten days of its life as a 'house' bee, the worker uses its wings to make flights outside the hive. As these flights are carried out, the bee tends each day to fly farther away, all the while learning how to locate the hive and get back home. It fixes the position of the hive in relation to neighbouring objects in the apiary site and the position of the sun in relation to these and the hive. It is now capable of becoming a forager or 'field' bee and younger bees take over the inside work.

The division of labour in a colony, according to the physiological age and ability of the worker bees to do the particular work, is not a rigid pattern. House bees are usually maids of all work, doing what is needed in the colony as they move about the broodnest. This is evident during a very good main nectar flow, when marked bees less than a week old will often be seen foraging. In the case of a hived swarm, quite old bees can cope with the feeding of young larvae.

The Drones are the largest bees in the colony. They are male bees, possess strong wings and are powerful flyers. Their sole function is to mate with the young virgin queen, and having done so they die. They cannot collect nectar or pollen nor do any work inside the hive. They have no sting and cannot even become guards. Drones are usually found in the colony from early May to mid-August. Once the mating season is over and the colony possesses a mated and laying queen, the drones are turned out of the hive to die. If a colony retains drones in autumn and winter it is usually a clear indication that the colony has either an unmated queen or is queenless.

Social Security in the Honeybee Colony. Social insects are members of a family in which the offspring and the mated female parent live in mutual co-operation in a common nest or shelter. This behaviour is possible because of the increased length of life of the parent and in the case of the queen honeybee it usually ensures the continuance of the social unit from one season to the next. The instinctive storing of food supplies and forming a cluster are essential to the successful overwintering of the colony. By swarming the social bee colony can reproduce itself.

In becoming social insects all three castes of the honeybee have lost the ability to live as individuals. A honeybee cannot survive for many hours when separated from the security of the colony. Within the community, through food interchange and sharing, there is freedom from hunger, a division of labour in food-gathering and brood-rearing, warmth in the bee cluster and collective defence of the social unit. The queen has become a specialized layer of eggs and provides the essential queen substance but has lost the ability to start up a home since she cannot make wax, rear brood or gather food as the solitary type of bee does. She has gained an increased length of life. The drone is not fitted to do any of the work inside or outside the hive and is simply a possible mate for a new queen. The female worker has lost the ability to mate and lay fertile eggs but has developed a specialized body and the ability to do the great variety of jobs needed for the maintenance of colony life. Organization, communications and behaviour patterns within the family are regulated by semi-automatic responses or instinctive reactions to the perceived stimuli of scents, vibrations, behaviour patterns,

11

dances and the chemicals in pheromones. Pheromones are very complex substances secreted and exuded by each individual bee (for example, queen substance, scents from the Nasonov and Kozhenikov glands, from sting poison and from developing brood) and they cause a definite behaviour or developmental reaction in other bees through their sense of smell, taste and touch.

MATERIALS USED BY HONEYBEES

Foraging duties are mainly concerned with gathering the materials needed for the well-being of the growing colony. These materials are nectar, pollen, water and propolis.

Nectar is a sweet liquid made by plants, usually scented and containing — according to the source and weather — from 15 per cent to 50 per cent of sugar in solution. Nectar exudes from nectaries at the base of most flowers and attracts insects who pollinate the flower as they seek the nectar source. The honeybee sucks nectar up through its specially constructed tube-like tongue and passes it into a honeysac inside its body. If it wants this energy-producing food itself it allows some to pass through a valve in the honeysac into the stomach where it is digested. If not, then it carries the nectar back to the hive, where it is disgorged into the cells or given to other bees to process into honey by evaporating the excess water and adding the glandular secretion, invertase. These changes from nectar into honey are called 'ripening'. Reliable estimates of the work involved by bees in collecting enough nectar to make 1 lb. of honey are illuminating. An average load in one honeysac is about 30 mg in weight. If the source of supply is half a mile from the hive then 1 lb. of honey would neces-sitate flights of between 45,000 and 50,000 miles by the bees working in aggregate.

Pollen is also gathered from flowers. As a bee crawls over the flowers the tiny pollen grains collect on the body hairs. Using its specially adapted legs, the bee cleans itself and packs the pollen into the pollen 'baskets' (*corbiculae*) on its third pair of legs. In the hive the pollen is mixed with nectar or honey to make 'bee bread' which is fed to developing larvae and eaten by young bees. The pollen supplies the essential body-building protein foods. If the pollen is not needed for instant use it is packed in cells and covered over with a little honey for use later. The loads of pollen carried by the bees are of different colours according to the kind of flower visited. Honeybees are usually 'flower faithful', gathering nectar and/or pollen from one variety of flower as long as the loads are worth while and the colony needs them. In spring beekeepers welcome the sight of worker bees returning to the hive with their loads of pollen, since this usually indicates that the queen has laid eggs to produce the larvae needing the protein food. A normal prosperous colony will use more than 60 lb. of pollen in a season. To gather this has meant visiting many millions of flowers. The work honeybees do in collecting pollen and so effectively fertilizing flowers to produce more and better fruit or seeds is important to fruit-growers and seed-producers.

Water is collected (in the same way as is nectar) for use in diluting stored honey when feeding it to larvae. It is also used in hot weather for evaporating inside the hive to reduce the hive temperature.

Propolis is the sticky, resinous substance collected by the bees from trees and shrubs. It is used as a kind of 'bee glue' to stop up cracks and fasten together the parts of the hive. Some strains of honeybees (especially Caucasians) also use it to build a barricade at the entrance of the hive.

Communications — Bee Dances. Foraging bees collect these four substances according to the demands for each within the colony. Worthwhile nectar (over 20 per cent sugar content) is always wanted and supplies of pollen are chiefly needed when there is a lot of brood to be fed.

On return to the hive with a profitable load, the forager will usually perform a dance to attract other bees as recruits. Von Frisch, who did years of research into the interpretation of these dances, found that there were two types — a round dance and a wag-tail figure-of-eight dance. These dances are

Diagram 2

BEE DANCES

ROUND DANCE
FOOD WITHIN 100 YARDS

WAGTAIL DANCE
FOOD BEYOND 100 YARDS

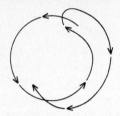

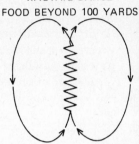

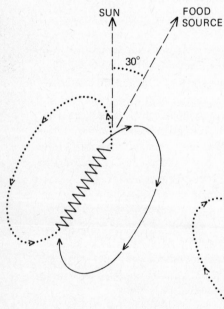

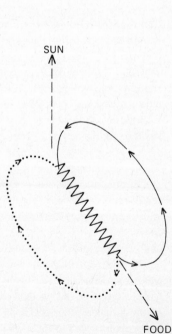

usually made on the vertical face of a hanging comb. (Diagram 2.)

The round dance (about 1½ in. diameter) usually indicates a source of supply within a hundred yards or so of the hive. Foragers with loads of pollen can often be seen doing this dance on a comb. The 'eagerness and quickness' with which they are relieved of their load (because it is needed by the colony) encourages them to continue gathering and, by dancing, to recruit others to the same task. When the load of pollen is ignored, then the forager 'loses interest' in the work, and rests until it is once again recruited for pollen- or nectar-gathering.

The intensity with which the dance is performed, its size, shape, number of turns and the number of tailwags made, together with the direction and duration of the straight run between two loops of the figure-of-eight dance, give accurate information to the recruited bees following the dance. Recruits have to learn how to keep in close touch with the dancer in the darkness of the hive. They also receive sips of the scented nectar carried by the dancing bee. In the figure-of-eight dance, the angle made by the straight-waggle run relative to the perpendicular on the comb shows the bearing of the sun's light when flying from the hive to the food source. A waggle run straight up the comb shows a source directly towards the sun's position at that time; straight down the comb means directly away from the sun's light. Much recent research and observation shows that the bearings indicated only have an error of 15 degrees, or less. The length of the run and the number of tailwags made show how far to fly. Recognition of the same nectar scent enables the recruited foragers to find the exact source of the nectar after flying the indicated distance.

This, then, is part of the language of bees — a language of dances. By interpretation, through an innate ability to understand the dance, recruited foragers could, without being led, fly from the hive straight to the source of supply.

RACES AND STRAINS OF HONEYBEES

Of the genus *Apis* (bee) there are several races, one of which, *Apis Mellifera* (honey-carrying bee) — sometimes referred to as *Apis Mellifica* (honey-making bee) — embraces nearly all the honeybees of the European mainland. Four varieties are easily distinguishable.

The *dark* bee of central and northern Europe includes the Dutch bee, the German brown bee, the French black bee and the original British bee. These dark bees are usually thrifty, hardy and are good comb-builders. In the case of the French strain the temper can be uncertain.

The *Carniolan* of Austria and the Balkans is a little smaller than other varieties and has a dark body with short thick grey hairs. The queens are large, copper-coloured and prolific. Carniolan bees are gentle and quiet on the combs but are much given to swarming.

The *Italian* bee of the Apennine region is distinguished by its yellow-banded abdomen and fawn-coloured hairs. It is docile and easily managed. The queens are prolific in brood-rearing but this, often carried on after the end of summer, can lead to excessive use of stores and poor wintering.

The *Caucasian* bee of the South Russian mountains is large, grey-haired and much given to using propolis. It is hardy, usually docile and is little given to swarming.

In Britain today, due to the importation of different varieties and strains, honeybees are mostly mongrels. It is difficult to find (or keep) any of the above races of bee in a pure form. In deciding which mixture of races to start with, it is advisable to find out which is best for your district by consulting successful beekeepers in the locality.

Establishment of an Apiary

Locality. As successful beekeeping depends so much on a suitable environment, this must be the first consideration. If bees are to thrive and to gather and store honey in excess of the needs of the colony, then the foraging bees must be able to work many acres of nectar-yielding flowers within a range of one mile from the hive. The nearer the apiary can be sited to the source of food supply the better, since foragers can then bring in more loads per hour in the spells of good weather and use less energy in flying.

Nectar flows. In most areas in Britain there are two main nectar flows — the spring-blossom flow and the main summer flow. In the spring the fruit trees (gooseberries, currants, raspberries, apples, pears and so on), together with sycamore and hawthorn, provide both nectar and pollen. The common dandelion is most valuable. Early supplies of pollen are also collected from catkin-bearing trees, crocuses and many early-flowering shrubs. At this season these fresh supplies of nectar and pollen are of the greatest value to the bee colony. The queen increases her rate of egg laying, more brood has to be fed and the resultant young bees will later become the foragers for the main flow.

To be ideal, the apiary site, as well as providing for a spring flow, must also provide for the gathering of copious supplies of nectar from the summer flows. Clover flowers are by far the most important midsummer source of nectar. Lime-tree blossom is another good source. Where large areas of special crops (field beans, sainfoin and so on) are grown it is often well worth while to move colonies to them and take advantage of the abundance of nectar produced. Each year in some fruit-growing areas, such as Kent, many hundreds of colonies are hired for placing in the orchards during blossom time. The improved weight and quality of the fruit, following the efficient pollination services of the bee, makes the hiring worth while. The same applies to the commercial production

17

of seed crops in other districts.

Although a surburban garden may offer the most convenient apiary site for the beekeeper, the surrounding area can seldom provide adequate forage for profitable beekeeping. One or two colonies may be able to support themselves but a useful surplus of honey cannot be gathered from gardens in a built-up area with its unproductive expanse of roads, roofs and well-cut lawns.

Another disadvantage is that neighbours often dislike the close proximity of colonies of bees.

What then is the answer? An *out-apiary*, within reasonable distance of home and carefully chosen to satisfy the requirements outlined above, is the practical solution. The bee colony does not require constant regular attention or feeding, and it is perfectly possible to have an efficient system of management involving only five or six visits during the active season from April to September.

After negotiation and agreement with the landowner, the work of establishing such an out-apiary is well rewarded by the increased pleasure when working with the bees and the greater possibility of surplus honey. Try to find a site away from any road or public footpath but with easy access to prevent a long carry of equipment. A site which is always dry and has some protection from the prevailing wind is most desirable. Avoid siting hives near overhanging branches of large trees. If there is no natural windbreak of bushes or hedge, a wicker screen can be erected. If a few hives are kept in a garden, the strategic placing of shrubs, wicker screens, or even tall plants can give protection and some, placed four or five feet from the hives in the flight paths, will cause the bees to fly above head height.

If on a farm, the whole apiary site should be protected from straying animals by using stout hedging stakes with two strands of barbed wire firmly fixed at about 18 in. and 30 in. above ground. Arrange in one place to have about 2 yd. of the top strand made with plain wire and removable for easy access.

The hives in an apiary should not be in a straight line with entrances all facing one way. They should be six or more feet apart and are best conveniently placed on a flat base raised some 9 in. to 18 in. above ground level. Convenient bases can be made of concrete paving slabs raised on bricks, or hive stands can be made using stout 3 in. x 2 in. timber. All hives must be perfectly level when in place.

It is an advantage if the whole apiary has a southerly aspect.

BUYING BEES

Having decided where you will keep your bees, and having gained advice from successful beekeepers in your locality, you will want to make a start. The month of May is a good time. There are several ways of obtaining bees:

A nucleus or small colony with worker bees covering four or five combs with brood, some stores and a young queen. A larger, overwintered colony with bees, brood and stores on eight to ten combs and with a young queen.

A swarm in early summer. This is a large number of bees from an established colony. It has no combs of brood or stores and usually has an older queen.

A package of bees with a queen in a queen cage.

It is essential in all cases that the adult bees and brood you buy are certified to be healthy and free from disease.

Colonies can be purchased from reputable bee-appliance firms but more often you will be able to make friends with a reliable, established beekeeper in your own area who will be able to supply your needs. This is to be recommended, and if you can arrange to watch and possibly help him when he is working with his colonies of bees during the previous summer, you can gain firsthand information about their docility and honey-producing qualities. In any case, you will find out if you like handling bees before incurring any expense in starting up as a beekeeper. Further help can be obtained from the local Beekeepers' Association and the County Beekeeping Adviser (see Appendix).

In starting with a nucleus the novice beekeeper can become used to handling bees and gain confidence and knowledge as the colony develops into full size. Little or no surplus honey can be expected in the first season. The larger colony soon becomes established and should give a surplus in a normal season. A swarm in late May or early June, if from a known source and healthy, is a quick way of establishing a colony. In good seasons it will often give a surplus of honey. The use of package bees is not recommended for the beginner.

Methods of establishing these colonies of bees in their hives are discussed on page 37.

CHAPTER 3
Beekeeping Equipment

CHOICE OF HIVE

All that the bee colony itself requires is a dry home, roomy enough to contain all the natural combs needed for brood-rearing and food-storage, and a way in and out.

The modern movable comb hive, while providing a most satisfactory home for the bees, also allows the beekeeper to carry out inspections, manipulations, extensions for honey storage and in fact all the operations needed to take the surplus honey without undue disturbance of the bee colony.

There are two kinds of hive used in Britain. The older kind (often called the W.B.C. after its designer W. B. Carr) has an outer casing around the rectangular boxes containing the colony and its combs.

The other kind is single-walled and does not require an outer casing. It is easier to transport, well adapted to suit modern systems of beekeeping, simple to make or assemble and has proved most efficient in use. Single-walled hives of varying sizes (see Table 2) are by far the most widely used in modern beekeeping throughout the world.

Basically, a single-walled hive will consist of a floor (usually reversible) with a detachable entrance block, a deep open-ended rectangular box to hold broodcombs (broodbox or broodchamber) and similar but shallower boxes (supers) to hold the combs of stored honey. A slotted excluder, through which worker bees can easily pass but not the larger-bodied queen or drone, is generally used to separate the part of the hive used by the queen and worker bees for brood-rearing from that part used for honey storage. On top is a coverboard and a flat weatherproof roof. By using additional boxes where and when required the beekeeper has both flexibility and interchangeability. Standardization of the type and size of hive used in an apiary is most desirable. Makeshifts and mixed kinds of hive make work.

Look through a few well-illustrated catalogues of bee

appliances and you will see the first major problem is in deciding which of the many available sizes of hive to use.

The shape and size of the open-ended box-like units which are used to make up a hive are determined by the size and number of frames to be used per box. To assist the bees in building even combs the beekeeper usually fits thin flat sheets of beeswax, embossed with a regular hexagonal cell base pattern, into the wooden frames. Bees readily use this as a foundation upon which to build the rows of cells on each side. The combs so built are kept a uniform distance apart in each box.

This distance is based on the fact that the natural 'worker brood' combs built by bees average $1\frac{3}{8}$ in. between centres but with combs used for honey storage the spacing may be as much as 2 in. It is essential to maintain the correct distance between the combs in the broodnest where worker brood-comb is needed. As yet, no method of achieving this is ideal or interchangeable. Two ways are commonly used:

'Metal end' spacers made of tinplate, punched out and folded so that they can be pushed on to the long lugs of the top bars of British Standard frames. Metal ends provide efficient and variable spacing but are tiresome to remove when firmly propolised to the lugs — and they have sharp edges.

'Hoffman' side bars on frames. This type of side bar has the upper two or three niches widened to make a shoulder giving a spacing of $1\frac{3}{8}$ in. The sides of the shoulder are shaped to minimize propolising by bees. Hoffman side bars have the merit that no other form of spacing is needed. They are generally used on frames which have short-lugged top bars. This method also has the advantage of helping to prevent combs from swinging against each other and so damaging combs and bees when the hive is being transported any distance.

Top or Bottom Beespace. A ¼ in. beespace is always allowed between the sides of the frames and the box and *either* at the bottom of the frames *or* above the frames. With a bottom beespace an unframed slotted sheet zinc excluder can be used but there is the disadvantage that the bees will often propolise the lugs of the frames to the junction between two boxes. With the top beespace this is less likely but the use of a rigidly framed excluder is necessary to prevent it from sagging in the centre.

Normally in the W.B.C. and National hives, bottom spacing is provided but in other types of hive top spacing is used.

Table 2 shows the various sizes of frames and hives. As the frame sizes include the thickness of wood used, the available comb areas given for one side of a framed comb are approximate. For comparison of the total available comb area in the different sizes of broodchamber this is based on frames made to British Standard specifications.

Among successful beekeepers each size and type of hive has its ardent advocates. It is essential that the size of brood-nest provided in the hive (that is, the total available brood-comb area whether in one or more broodboxes) must suit the needs of the strain of bee to be used in your district and also your method of management. A prolific strain of queen need-ing a large broodnest would be uneconomic in an area with limited sources of nectar and only one good summer every five years, but would suit another area known to have good nectar flows and consistently good summer weather. The district and weather conditions in average summers must in-fluence the choice of the best strain of bee and thus the size of broodnest to be provided in the hive.

The size of broodframe in general use throughout Britain is known as the British Standard (often abbreviated to 'B.S.') frame. The one used most in America, Canada and Australasia, to suit the more prolific strain of bee used in the better climatic conditions with copious regular nectar flows, is the Langstroth. Where colony management is based on having the broodnest in one large broodchamber the Modified Dadant can be used.

In Britain, my own choice is the B.S. frame used in the Modified National hive. The hives, constructed of cedarwood and treated externally with non-toxic wood preservative

23

Table 2. **COMPARISON OF BEEHIVES IN COMMON USE**

HIVE PATTERN		External Size of Box Units (In Inches) L	W	D	Number of Combs	Size of Frames (In Inches) Top Bar	W	D	Comb Area One Side (Sq. Ins.)	Total Comb Area in a Brood Box (Both Sides of Combs)	Equivalent Number of British Standard Combs
W.B.C.	BB	$17\frac{3}{4}$	16	$8\frac{7}{8}$	10	17	14	$8\frac{1}{2}$	99 to 104	1988	10
Double Walled	SS	$17\frac{3}{4}$	16	$5\frac{7}{8}$	∝	17	14	$5\frac{1}{2}$	59 to 63	—	
Modified	BB	$18\frac{1}{8}$	$18\frac{1}{8}$	$8\frac{7}{8}$	11	17	14	$8\frac{1}{2}$	99 to 104	2186	11
National	SS	$18\frac{1}{8}$	$18\frac{1}{8}$	$5\frac{7}{8}$	∝	17	14	$5\frac{1}{2}$	59 to 63	1320 (11 Combs)	6·6
Smith	BB	$18\frac{1}{4}$	$16\frac{3}{8}$	$8\frac{7}{8}$	11	$15\frac{1}{2}$	14	$8\frac{1}{2}$	99 to 104	2186	11
	SS	$18\frac{1}{4}$	$16\frac{3}{8}$	$5\frac{7}{8}$	∝	$15\frac{1}{2}$	14	$5\frac{1}{2}$	59 to 63	—	
Modified British	BB	$18\frac{5}{16}$	$18\frac{5}{16}$	$10\frac{1}{2}$	11	$17\frac{1}{4}$	16	10	138	3020	15·1
Commercial	SS	$18\frac{5}{16}$	$18\frac{5}{16}$	$6\frac{3}{8}$	∝	$17\frac{1}{4}$	16	6		—	
Langstroth	BB	20	$16\frac{1}{4}$	$9\frac{9}{16}$	10	19	$17\frac{5}{8}$	$9\frac{1}{8}$	138	2742	13·8
	SS	20	$16\frac{1}{4}$	$5\frac{3}{4}$	∝	19	$17\frac{5}{8}$	$5\frac{3}{8}$		—	
Modified	BB	20	$18\frac{1}{2}$	$11\frac{3}{4}$	11	19	$17\frac{5}{8}$	$11\frac{1}{4}$	173	3805	19·1
Dadant	SS	20	$18\frac{1}{2}$	$6\frac{5}{8}$	∝	19	$17\frac{5}{8}$	$6\frac{1}{4}$		—	

... same as for broodbox, or varied to suit a wider spacing for thick

when made, have been in use for over thirty years. Usually, if bought assembled, the beespace in the broodbox and super-boxes is provided below the frames. I prefer this beespace to be above the frames. By using a single broodbox, or broodbox and super-box, or two broodboxes, or even two or three super-boxes (for less weight to lift) one can achieve maximum flexibility and suit the size of broodnest to the needs of the colony and its queen.

The Smith hive affords the same flexibility and comb capacity. It is cheaper and simpler in construction because short-lugged (¾ in. instead of 1½ in.) top bars are used on the Standard frames. The broodbox has top beespacing. Modified National and Smith hives are both efficient in use and easy to transport.

If the merits of using larger frames (short-lugged) in a single broodbox are considered all important then there is the Modified Commercial hive. As it has bottom beespacing and is very little larger in length and width it can be used on a Modified National floor and will take National broodboxes and shallow boxes as upper honey supers. The same ex-cluders, crownboards and roof can be used.

Nucleus Hives, holding five combs of the same frame size as those used in the hives in the apiary, are essential for queen-rearing, swarm-control and many other manipulations in beekeeping. The nucleus body-box can be made by cutting a broodbox in half and adding sides, detachable floor, cover-board and roof.

Other Essential Equipment includes a smoker (preferably the bent-nose type), a hive tool and covercloths. Covercloths (18 in. x 20 in.) can be conveniently made from old deck-chair canvas. For extracting honey from the honeycombs of supers an extractor, strainer and settling tank will be needed.

Personal Protection. For personal protection you will need a net veil with a wide brim to keep it from touching your face and fitted with elastic or tapes to secure it round your chest and so stop bees from crawling inside. Sleeves and trouser legs should be secured by stout elastic bands, string or clips. Better still use a light-coloured boiler suit (dungarees) and Wellington boots. At first you may wish to use gloves but dispense with them as soon as you can. At the best of times they make handling more difficult.

Beekeeping Box. This can be a light box with rope handles, a basket, or holdall. In it you can keep the smoker, spare fuel refills of corrugated cardboard or sacking, gloves, hive tool and several covercloths. To these might be added: a few spare metal ends if used, pieces of perforated zinc to cover feed-holes, a queen cage with candy, a queen-introduction cage, some sugar syrup in a bottle with a firm screw top, a tin for odd bits of comb or wax, another screw-top tobacco tin containing drawing-pins, bradnails, useful screws and hive staples, a stout envelope in which to keep a few postcards and a pencil sharpened at both ends, some empty matchboxes (with elastic bands) and one with matches. A lidded honey jar containing a subduing-cloth (one sprinkled with drops of benzaldehyde or dilute carbolic) can be included for use in clearing bees away from combs when deemed necessary. Such a box of useful oddments will save many a trip back to the garage or bee shed and is most useful when at an out-apiary.

Feeders will have to be used in any apiary when colonies are in need of sustenance. Emergency feeding in spring; autumn feeding to augment natural honey stores for winter-ing; feeding to help a small colony or swarm to develop to full size are all necessary at some time or other. Rapid feeders holding four to eight pints can be bought but are easily made from a large tin with a wide recessed lever-top lid. Many such tins are being used for powdered foodstuffs. To make it into a satisfactory feeder, take the lid and place it (inner side up) on a block of wood. Using an 18-gauge nail (panel pin) punch about twenty fine holes in it. Arrange the holes evenly within a 2½ in. circle in the centre of the lid. The tin is filled to the top with sugar syrup (2 lb. to 1 pint) and the lid pressed firmly in place. When required the feeder is quickly inverted over the feed-hole in the coverboard. The recessed flange of the lid gives the bees access to the drops of syrup at the holes.

The partial vacuum inside the tin prevents the syrup from running out. Feeders need to be surrounded by an empty super or broodbox to raise the roof clear of the tin.

Avoid spilling syrup (possible cause of robbing) and feed whenever possible in the late evening.

BOARDS: COVER-, CROWN-, CLEARER, MULTI-PURPOSE

A *coverboard or crownboard* is a board to cover tops of the frames in the uppermost box in a hive. Around the edges on the underside there is a rebate (1¼ in. wide by ¼ in deep) to provide a beeway passage over the tops of the frames. It usually has a central feed-hole shaped to take a 'bee escape' when it is used for clearing bees from honey super-boxes.

The *clearer board* is an improved coverboard usually with similar rebates on both sides and with two or more holes for bee escapes and often with a return hole covered with a thin metal slide.

The *multipurpose board* (the MP board) is a further simple adaptation of a clearer board which I devised for use when raising and mating young replacement queens in nuclei on top of a single-walled hive. Details of the adaptation are shown in Diagram 7 on page 60 and its use is fully described in later chapters. When entrances in the MP board are being used by bees, it is advisable to provide an alighting-platform. A piece of perforated zinc about the size of a postcard is pushed under the entrance used by the bees in between the MP board and the edge of the box on which it rests. This piece of zinc is bent slightly down to make a small sloping alighting-platform. If coloured in a broad pattern of stripes or other design it also serves as an orientation mark for returning young queens and bees. Different colours and markings can be used for platforms at the different entrances.

Bee Escapes are devices fitted into the holes in a clearer board and only allow a one-way traffic of bees. The bees in the honey supers must go through one of these escapes to get to the broodnest and entrance and cannot get back. Two or three such escapes in a clearer board are better than one which may get blocked up. The clearer board is placed under one or two full honey supers and in good flying weather they will have been cleared of bees in about thirty-six hours. The two-exit Porter bee escape was the original type and the eight-exit Crowther escape is a modern improvement.

ROOF

A colony of honeybees needs a dry home. It is essential that the hive roof is weatherproof and that four strips of wood are fixed inside round the top to give a ventilated beeproof 1½" headspace above the crownboard.

In the next chapter (p. 32, 4.) during an inspection of a colony the hive roof when removed is used as a flat topped table on which to place the honey super or broodchamber. This can be done provided the super or broodchamber has a bottom beespace (p.22) and there is little danger of crushing some bees but when using equipment that has top bee-spacing, the roof should be placed with the open end upwards. The super or broodchamber can then be placed with the corners resting on the sides of the upturned roof and there is no danger of crushing any bees. The gabled roof of the W.B.C. type of hive has to be used in this way.

The perusal of an up-to-date well illustrated catalogue of beekeeping supplies will provide the reader with full details of all equipment.

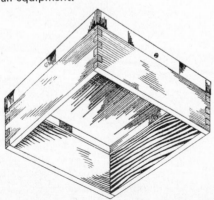

CHAPTER 4
Working with Bees in the Apiary

If by practice you can learn how to handle bees at all times with confidence and assurance and combine with this a knowledge of their instinctive reactions, behaviour and activities you will have gained something that neither books nor lectures can teach you. By watching and noting the way experts 'open up' and diagnose colonies when demonstrating with bees, you can see the orderly routine followed after the 'smoking'.

Effect of Smoke. Honeybees' reaction to smoke is instinctive. It is a survival factor inherited from those primeval times when the smoke from oncoming forest fires warned colonies of wild bees to evacuate their home and prepare for a journey in search of a new home, much as a swarm does before emergence. Those bees that did not react to the warning smell of smoke died. Honeybees, when warned by smoke, engorge honey or nectar from their stores, taking a few minutes to fill their honeysacs with enough to last for several days if required.

Consider the following important points before using smoke to subdue the colony.

1. Unless the bees have immediate access to unsealed stores in the broodnest, the smoking will only cause them to rush about the combs agitated and in a stinging mood instead of having their heads in cells as they quickly imbibe nectar or honey. Bees do not readily uncap sealed stores; it takes time and is only usual when they are feeding brood with over-wintered stores in early spring. First, then, look at the alighting-board or entrance to see if there is debris from uncapped stores so used. Test the weight of the hive by a gentle lift from the back and if you are then uncertain of their stores, give a small cupful of sugar syrup dribbled through the feed-hole some few minutes before smoking the colony.

2. Are the bees flying strongly from the entrance and so indicating that the weather is right?

3. Is the opening up really necessary? What exactly do you expect to find? What might you find? What precisely will you do? Have you an operational plan (and equipment) to meet and deal with any eventuality?

4. Have you everything you may need for manipulation and also to put the colony right, after diagnosis, until the next inspection? — beekeeping box, nucleus hive, spare super and combs, a few broodframes filled with foundation and, if thought needed, supplies for emergency feeding.

5. Have you complete personal protection? Do not risk a limp net veil negligently tucked in your jacket lapels — it may come adrift. The middle of an operation is not the time to find that you have to put on your glasses to inspect a comb.

6. Finally, after duly checking all these points, light the smoker fuel and get it going well. A smoker kept upright will usually keep alight — on its side it goes out.

7. Use a method of 'cross-fire' smoking. The smoke going into the entrance along the floor to the side walls clears the bees from the outside combs, one of which you will first want to handle. The queen will usually move to the central combs away from the smoke. Smoke, if blasted into the central combs of the broodnest, will make the bees and queen move to the right and/or left flanks, leaving the young brood temporarily uncovered by bees and making the outside combs more difficult to handle. (Diagram 3 b.).

Throughout your manipulations cultivate a calm, deliberate gentleness with no jarring or crushing of bees (this sets off the alarm signals from the scent of bee-sting venom). Adopt a routine for opening up a colony. Put each hive part in its best place, leaving a space at back and sides for your feet.

SPRING INSPECTION AND CLEANING

The colony you are about to inspect may have overwintered in a single broodchamber, a broodchamber with a shallow box of combs as an extension, or two broodchambers. On top of any of these honey supers may have been stored.

I will commence with the simplest of these — the single

Diagram 3b. **USING A SMOKER**

OF A BROODCOMB

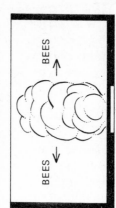

(i) COMB POSITION WHEN REMOVED FROM BROODNEST

(ii) POSITION AFTER LOWERING R. HAND AND RAISING L. HAND

(iii) POSITION AFTER TURNING THE COMB THROUGH A HALF-CIRCLE AWAY FROM YOU

(iv) THE OTHER SIDE IN VIEW BY LOWERING L. HAND AND RAISING R. HAND

OPERATION ALWAYS TO BE DONE OVER THE BROODNEST. REVERSE OPERATION FOR RETURN TO (i)

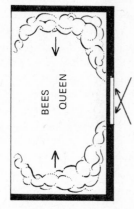

BEES
BEES

SMOKE USED THIS WAY SPLITS THE BROODNEST BEES MOVE TO SIDEWALLS. QUEEN MOVES EITHER RIGHT OR LEFT.

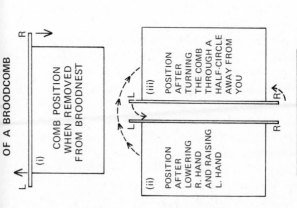

BEES
QUEEN

"CROSS FIRE" SMOKING

BROODNEST NOT SPLIT. BEES CLEARED FROM SIDEWALLS. QUEEN SAFE IN CENTRE. FIRST SIDE COMB EASIER TO REMOVE.

broodchamber on its floor with a coverboard on top and a roof over all. It is good weather in mid or late April. Bees are flying well and perhaps bringing in early nectar and pollen. The sight of pollen-bearers alighting at the entrance will mean that brood is likely to be in the broodcombs from eggs laid by the queen. In addition to the usual items of equipment you will have brought an excluder (if one was not already on the hive), a honey super, preferably with drawn-out combs, and the empty nucleus hive. If you have a spare clean floor this will help to speed up the operation.

Proceed as follows:

1. Decide which side you will work from so that the light is at your back — but if the bees seem to be going in at only one side of the entrance (showing where the broodnest is likely to be) choose the other side where the first combs handled will have less bees on them.

2. Use cross-fire smoking, two good puffs to the right along the floor and two to the left. Then pause for a minute or two while the bees instinctively fill up with honey.

3. Place the nucleus hive (roof and coverboard removed) in a convenient position near the hive to receive the first (outside) comb.

4. Take hold of the bottom edges of the roof with your hands at the diagonal corners and, using the little fingers as guides, lift it vertically up and off without jarring the broodchamber. Place the roof on the side opposite to the nucleus box so that the flat top can be used as a table on which to put the honey super and its combs.

5. Holding the broodchamber and floor at the base, gently move it a few feet to one side or in front. On the original site place the clean floor. Now, using the hive tool with care, free the broodchamber from its floor. Insert the flat thin blade at the corners, use very little leverage and avoid any sudden jerk. When you can see that it is free, lift the broodchamber on to the new floor still with the coverboard on and the bees quiet on the combs. If there are many bees on the old floor (unusual) put it in front of the new entrance so that they can run in.

6. Again using the hive tool free the coverboard in the same way. Before lifting it off give it a controlled ¾ in. twist to left and right. This will break any adhering propolis or bracecomb. Raise the back of the crownboard just an inch, and see that no combs are being lifted up. Give a few gentle puffs of smoke over the tops of the combs. If any combs are being lifted, gently push them down with the hive tool.

7. When the board is free, lift it off by turning it up and over from the back and then put it 'bee side' up in front of the hive entrance so that any bees on it can run back into the broodnest.

8. Now gently spread a covercloth over the broodcombs and bees, leaving only the one against the side wall exposed.

9. Gently free this comb and, holding the ends of the frame (lugs), raise it slowly and vertically out of the brood-nest. Note by weight and sight if it has stores in it. Put it in the nucleus hive for safety and cover it with a cloth or the nucleus coverboard. Move the cloth over the broodnest and expose the next comb. Gently separate it from the adjacent one and move it into the gap made by removing the first comb. It can now be raised vertically and examined over the broodnest (in case bees and/or the queen fall off). Diagram 3 a shows how to move a comb, without changing hands, in order to see both sides and yet keep the comb in a vertical plane.

10. What will you look for? The presence of eggs, pearly white glistening larvae, or normal regular sealed worker brood will show that the queen has been at work and for how long. The amount of stores left should also be noted. When you note eggs and very young larvae in the cells of a comb, be particularly careful for, although you may not see the queen, this is the most likely place for her to be. Look round the perimeter of a comb face first in case she may be going round to the other side. Hold the comb about 18 in. from your eyes so that you can see it as a whole. After practice you will only notice drones and the queen (because of their size) against the background of worker bees on the comb. Do not hunt for the queen, but if you should see her, make certain she has moved to a position of safety in the middle of the face of the comb

Photograph 3 A comb of brood, bees and arch of sealed honey.

before you put it back. If she is on the bottom or side of a
comb there is danger of her being dislodged and harmed when
replacing it. Put the comb carefully back into the gap and
then slide it towards the side wall so that a new gap is made
for raising the next comb. Using a comb-space gap in this way
prevents rubbing bees against bees and possibly causing the
queen to fall to the floor. It is essential for the quiet handling
of bees and makes the finding of the queen, when need be,
easier and more likely. Proceed with each comb similarly,
covering those already inspected with another covercloth. In
this way only one comb is exposed at a time and the bees are
kept under control. Having examined all the combs, noted
any that are poor and need replacement and made an assess-
ment of the colony as a whole, move them together so that
the first comb may be put back. If there are any bees left
on the crownboard or nucleus box, take off the covercloth
and shake them into the colony on the tops of the combs.

11. Now take out your subduing-cloth from the honey jar in the beekeeping box. This cloth is put on over the tops of the combs instead of a covercloth. The smell and vapour of the benzaldehyde (or carbolic) cause bees to retreat. It must not be too strong, about twenty drops sprinkled evenly over a 20 in. square is usually efficient. In fifteen to twenty seconds the bees will have left the tops of the combs. Take the cloth away. You can then scrape the top bars and remove any bracecomb with the hive tool. Put the scrapings in the tin you have, do not throw them on the ground. Do this scraping smoothly, and always without force. Avoid digging the sharp hive tool into the top bar. If the bees start to come up, put the subduing-cloth on again for some few seconds.

12. Having cleaned the frame tops, put on the excluder. The slots or wires must go across the frames. The honey super lifted from the flat roof table is now placed on the excluder with the combs in it running the same way as those in the broodchamber below. Now put on the original crownboard. It may need some scraping to remove bracecomb. If a winter mouse guard was covering the original entrance, a normal entrance block can now replace it.

13. Before putting on the roof make a note on a card. It might read as follows: 20/4/74, No. 1 hive, Stores 12 lb., E, L, SB, DB. Q seen, Bees 7c. (Eggs, larvae, sealed worker and drone brood present, queen was seen, bees covered 7 combs.) Subsequent notes may show the relative amounts (areas) of brood and the presence of drones. Pin this card on the crownboard, then put on the roof using the same technique as when lifting it off. Finally, before leaving the hive, check that it is reassembled correctly and that you have done what was needed. Make a note when you should next inspect it and what you might then have to do.

When carrying out other beekeeping operations during the active season, many additional manipulations will of necessity have to be fitted in to the above basic routine.

14. If at this spring inspection you had no spare floor then the broodchamber when freed from its floor would be gently placed on the flat roof. The floor cleaned and/or

reversed is put back on the original site and then the brood-chamber lifted back on it. Items taken from the first hive can be made ready for use with the next — if hives are of one standard pattern and the bees are healthy.

15. A flat roof from another hive will provide an extra table when required. When inspecting a colony in two brood-boxes (broodbox and super or two broodboxes) and with perhaps three supers with honey and bees in them, you will need to use two roof tables for ease and efficiency. After subduing, remove the top two supers (see basic routine 6) together with crownboard on top, to one table. The third super, covered with a cloth, is put on top of these. All the bees in these supers are confined and will go on working and not fly back to cause congestion in the broodnest. The top box of the broodnest, after removal of excluder (put in front bee side up), is covered with a cloth and put on the other roof table. Basic routine inspection of the bottom box on its floor (or new floor) now follows. This is left covered with a cover-cloth while the upper broodbox on the roof table is examined. After examination it is replaced back in position, the excluder put on, and then the supers. If the supers need rearrangement or another one added this can be done before putting them back.

16. If the operation is only a simple one involving the addition of an extra super and no broodnest inspection, there is no need to disrupt the work in the broodnest with smoke. Give a puff of smoke *across* the entrance to make the guard bees run inside. Take off the roof, put the new super on it. Remove the crownboard (basic routine 6), put it on top of the new super and immediately put both back on the hive. This need only take a minute. Diagram 4 shows methods of supering.

Plan each operation before commencing it. The routine spring inspection described assumes that you are dealing with a normal healthy colony with adequate stores. Problems of emergency feeding, of abnormalities found during the inspection and diagnosis of the broodnest are dealt with in later chapters.

HIVING A PURCHASED NUCLEUS OR COLONY

Nucleus colonies are delivered in special travelling-boxes which have wire gauze in the lid for ventilation. The bumps and shakes of the journey demoralize the bees and they are hot and thirsty, so first put the box in a cool shady place. Make some thin sugar syrup — a cupful of cold water with a piled dessertspoonful of sugar dissolved in it. Dribble a spoonful at a time along the wire gauze (see the bees' tongues lick it up). Then leave them to quieten down till late afternoon or early evening.

Prepare the hive with the single broodchamber on its floor and with the entrance block providing only a small 2 in. entrance. In the broodchamber you will have placed two frames fitted with new foundation and a dummy or division board. This board is used to restrict the size of the brood-nest — a kind of internal movable side wall. The crownboard, with central feed-hole open and any others covered with perforated zinc, can be laid in front of the hive and the roof placed as a table close to the broodbox. Put the travelling-box containing the four- or five-comb nucleus on the flat roof. Blow a little smoke through the ventilating screen. Pause. Arrange to have one frame in the broodbox next to the side wall. Undo and lift off the top of the travelling-box. Shake any bees on it into the broodbox. Transfer the combs of bees one by one to the hive, making sure they are placed in the same order and relative positions as they were when in the travelling-box. Check the combs to see that they contain brood in all stages and a balanced amount of food. British Standard Specification requires: a laying queen, no visible signs of disease, worker brood of all stages covering at least half the comb area, over 1 lb. of honey and pollen per comb and sufficient bees to fully cover all the combs. You may see the queen but do not spend time in searching for her. Then, checking that she is not amongst the bees left in the box, shake them into one corner and then into the broodbox on top of the combs. If she was in the box, coax her out on to the combs before shaking in the bees. Place the other frame of foundation next to the last comb and then the dummy

37

board. (Comb order should now be: side wall, FCCCCF, division board, space, side wall.) Put on the coverboard and a feeder with three or four pints of syrup (2 lb. to 1 pint) prepared in readiness beforehand. Put on an empty super-box so that the roof, when put back, will not rest on the feeder. Check the entrance and make certain the bees can use it. At the next inspection (using basic routines) you will probably find that the foundation is being drawn out into comb. If this is so, add one more frame of foundation, putting it in between an outside comb and its neighbour. Feeding must be continued and frames of foundation added in this manner until all are drawn out and the much-enlarged colony can gather enough nectar to support itself.

Treated in this way, such a purchased nucleus colony may become full-sized before the end of June. A super can be added over an excluder (basic routine 12). If the super is fitted with frames of foundation only, then it is advisable to give another syrup feed to encourage the bees to draw out the wax foundation. No feeding should be given when honey is being stored in the supers.

When installing an eight-comb colony use the same plan. After its journey it will take a couple of cups of thin cold syrup. When setting up the hive, leave the broodchamber empty. Give an entrance with normal opening. Transfer the combs (in correct order) to the hive, the extra three frames of foundation being added last and placed in between the out-side comb and its neighbour (CFFCCCCCCFC). Again feed. Such a colony should quickly establish itself and a super can be given after a week or ten days. Frames of foundation in a super should always be on narrow ($1\frac{3}{8}$ in.) spacing until drawn out.

HIVING A SWARM

A swarm may be hived by a direct rapid method or allowed to run in through the hive entrance. The first way is easy and quick, the second most interesting to watch. The swarm may be delivered in a skep (a straw hive) or a box and should be kept in a cool shady place until near sunset.

Hiving direct. Put the hive floor, with normal entrance

block, on its base with an *empty* super or broodbox on it. On the hive roof table place the broodchamber with its full complement of narrowly spaced frames fitted with foundation. (If you have a few spare 'clean' drawn-out combs to put in the centre it will be an advantage since the queen will be able to lay eggs in these without waiting for bees to draw out foundation.) On this will be the crownboard and covered feeder with three or four pints of sugar syrup. The skep, or box, containing the swarm is brought alongside the hive, the covering quietly removed and then the skep, 'mouth' downwards, held over the empty super-box and the swarm 'dumped' in. This is done with a sudden jerk which causes the bees to fall down in a mass. Quickly put the prepared broodchamber on top of the super-box, now full of crawling bees, and put on the roof.

The bees in the swarm will soon run up into the broodbox above and start drawing out the foundation. Next day the empty box below can be removed and the broodchamber put on the hive floor.

In a few days make a routine inspection. Most probably you will find that the bees do not cover all the frames in the box. Move the occupied frames to one side of the box and close off the other side and the unoccupied frames by using a division board. Management now follows the same pattern as with the purchased nucleus.

Running in a swarm at the entrance. Place the prepared broodchamber with its complement of frames fitted with foundation (and possibly one or two combs in the centre) on its floor, in position, but with entrance block removed to give a wide open entrance. The crownboard, feeder with surrounding empty super and roof will be in position. A wide flat board is now placed so that it slopes from the ground right up to and touching the entrance. It must be secure and not block the entrance. Over this board and spreading out to the sides and beyond the board a sheet of calico (or old sheeting) is stretched. Secure it with stones. The whole forms a gentle slope up which the shaken or dumped swarm will march into the hive. The dumping is done as described above but on to

39

the sheet. You may see the queen going in. There must be no gap between the slope and the open entrance. Instinctively moving uphill, the bees will soon commence marching and as soon as the queen has gone in, if not before, many bees will be seen busily fanning with their wings, legs apart and with the tips of their abdomens in the air. They are giving off a scent from their Nasonov scent gland and thus calling all other bees to come to the new home. You can actually smell this scent — it is something like nail varnish. When all are in, the normal entrance block can be replaced and the sheet and board removed. Compared with the direct method, this running in of a swarm is slow — often taking over an hour — but should be seen at least once by every beekeeper.

Subsequent management — reduction of number of frames to those occupied by the swarm, giving room for development by adding a frame at a time, and feeding — follows the same routine as with the first method.

BEE STINGS

If bees are handled with care, confidence and gentleness in good conditions there will be few occasions when they will want to use their stings on the beekeeper. The smell of the sting poison from a crushed bee can alert other bees. Bee stings are usually painful at first and are often accompanied by a localized swelling. The first thing to do when stung by a bee is to scrape the sting away with a fingernail or hive tool. This action, done immediately after the stinging, lessens the amount of the poison injected. By directing some smoke from the smoker on to the stung part of the skin, the smell of the poison can be deodorized. Some 'anti-sting' ointments are effective if used immediately on the spot which has been stung. Any serious reaction — considerable swelling and/or faintness — should be attended to by a doctor. You may be allergic to bee stings.

It cannot be emphasized enough that full personal protection, particularly the efficient, well-secured veil, should always be worn, and until you are experienced, rubber gloves, gauntlets and rubber boots are an added protection.

Spring is nature's season of growth. In a healthy bee colony the advent of the warmer weather and the incoming supplies of fresh pollen and nectar stimulate brood-rearing. Spring management centres around the provision of adequate room for this expansion. At this time the broodnest must always be a place where the queen has no restriction on her rate of laying. There must be ample room in empty worker cells before she needs to use them. Congestion of the brood-nest with incoming nectar often causes harmful birth control. The putting on of a super of drawn-out combs *early* in spring to provide storage room for the surplus nectar is most important. When bees have started storing nectar in the broodnest and have enlarged the cells on the tops of the broodcombs, it is already too late. Room for the storage of nectar and honey must always be provided in advance of the colony's requirements.

When using a single B.S. broodchamber a regular check must be made to make certain that the broodnest does not become congested. It must be an 'open' broodnest — lack of room and restriction of egg-laying are all precursors of 'forced' swarming (see chapter 6). Again, if the necessary combs in the single broodchamber are kept open for egg-laying, provision must be made in a super for a reserve of stores for use by the colony in a bad spell of weather in spring. More colonies are lost through starvation in early spring than through any bee disease. Such difficulties do not occur in well-founded colonies in *large* single broodchambers or in those in two boxes.

ROOM FOR EXPANSION IN THE BROODNEST

In cases where the beekeeper's system of management demands that the broodnest has to be confined in a single broodchamber and no extensions involving the use of a second chamber can be considered, there is a method of relieving congestion in the broodnest when it occurs. This entails using an MP board (Diagram 7a) on top of the hive (or on another hive). On top of this MP board an empty broodchamber is placed. Two or three of the combs causing the congestion in the broodnest (overwintered and unrequired honey stores, poor combs with some stores or too much drone brood, combs with mouldy pollen, and some containing only sealed or emerging worker brood) are put into this top broodchamber and are replaced using empty combs or frames of foundation. A careful check must be made to make certain that the queen is left in the broodnest. An inspection of another colony may show that two such combs should be replaced. These two can also be placed alongside those already in the upper box. Then, having relieved the congestion in several broodnests in this way, the combs of stores, sealed brood and adhering bees are moved together using a division board to close off the unoccupied space. A crownboard is used to cover this broodchamber. The MP board will have had the central feed-hole and any other bee-escape holes covered with pinned-down pieces of excluder. Normally, the bees will mix with those coming up from the super below quite amicably and the transferred brood (all sealed) will hatch out into young bees in about a fortnight. If the bees should show any signs of fighting, sprinkle them and the combs liberally with thin sugar syrup (from the bottle carried in the beekeeping box). If there were many drones to hatch out, open the rear entrance in the MP board after about a week. In double-walled hives (W.B.C. type) the roof would have to be removed and the crownboard lifted to release the drones. This done at the end of a week and again every four or five days would prevent the drones from being trapped in trying to get through the excluders in the MP board. When all the brood has hatched out, any bees remaining on the combs can be cleared by putting bee escapes in the holes in the MP board in place of the pieces of excluder. The combs, if suitable, can be re-used or kept for later use in nuclei when queen-rearing is carried out.

Diagram 4

BUILDING OF DRAWN-OUT COMB
SINGLE BROODCHAMBER IN USE

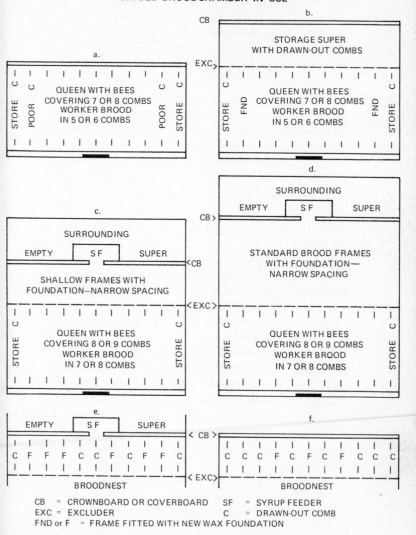

CB = CROWNBOARD OR COVERBOARD   SF = SYRUP FEEDER
EXC = EXCLUDER   C = DRAWN-OUT COMB
FND or F = FRAME FITTED WITH NEW WAX FOUNDATION

EXTENDING THE BROODNEST

In any extension of the broodnest by the adding of a second chamber, the frames/combs in the added upper box *must* have the same *narrow spacing* as those in the broodchamber and must be placed vertically over those below. Wherever frames of foundation are being drawn out they must be narrowly spaced, otherwise the bees will build an additional natural comb in between them.

1. In mid-May if the overwintered colony fully occupies a single broodchamber (as in Diagram 4a) you can provide more room for the broodnest by adding a shallow super-box fitted with narrow-spaced combs or a mixture of combs and frames fitted with foundation. The arrangement should finish as in Diagrams 4c, 4e, or 4f according to the availability of suitable good clean worker combs but without an excluder between the two boxes.

2. Similarly a second standard-size broodchamber can be added as shown in Diagrams 5b or 5c. In this case it will be noted that three combs of stores, brood and bees have been moved from the bottom box into the top box. Throughout handle all moved combs with great care, as the queen, not seen, may be on one of them in either box. No excluder is between the two boxes. During subsequent inspections of the top box, move in the frames with foundation, one at a time, as they become drawn out.

In both the above operations (1 and 2) some feeding with sugar syrup will usually be necessary and this should be done before any supers for honey storage are in place.

Water. Often in early March, long before the supplies of watery nectar come in, honey from stores has to be diluted with water. If there is no near-by convenient source of clean water, it is a good plan to provide one. A large shallow bowl or bath, with clean sacking draped around the inside and over the edges and kept supplied with water, can be used. See that it is not in the flight path in front of the hives, or too near, where any voided excreta from flying bees could foul the water. The wet sacking and pieces of thin wood floating on the surface of the water provide landing-places for the water-foraging bees and prevent losses through drowning.

Diagram 5

EXTENDING THE BROODNEST

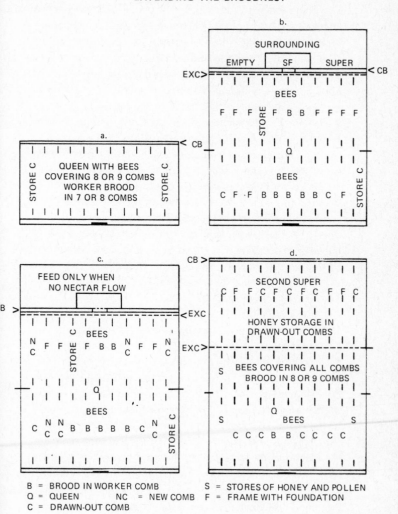

B = BROOD IN WORKER COMB   S = STORES OF HONEY AND POLLEN
Q = QUEEN   NC = NEW COMB   F = FRAME WITH FOUNDATION
C = DRAWN-OUT COMB

REVERSING BROODCHAMBERS

About mid-May, or even a week or so earlier according to the season, many colonies, overwintered with broodnests in two boxes (standard broodbox and shallow extension or two standard broodchambers) will have fully used the top box for brood-rearing and have started in the one below (Diagram 5d). Expansion of the broodnest can be encouraged by reversing the two boxes and then replacing any broodless poor combs with frames fitted with foundation. The final arrangement should be as in Diagram 6d with the bottom box a shallow or standard box according to the method of over-wintering.

If the broodnest of the colony was originally in a standard broodchamber and a shallow box as the extension you will now have only the standard size of broodcombs in the acces-sible top box to inspect during the rest of the season. Seldom is it found necessary to go through the shallow bottom box. This is particularly so when the colony is headed by a young queen of good strain in her first full season. Towards the end of the summer flow of nectar, at the end of July, the boxes will again be reversed. (See chapter 6.)

ADDING SUPERS

Quick inspections of the first super can be made without disorganizing the work going on in the broodnest (chapter 4: basic routine 16). Check the storage of honey in the combs in the first super-box. The central combs are usually the first filled and sealed. When five or six are full and sealed, or nearly so, rearrange the combs, putting those that are full and sealed to the flanks and moving the empty or partly filled ones to the centre (as in Diagrams 6a and 6b). At the same time add the second super on top. When honey is being stored in this second super, put it below the first next to the excluder.

Shortage of drawn-out comb is always experienced when beginning beekeeping. If you want to add second supers to two hives but have only one spare set of shallow combs, make up the two super-boxes as shown in the second super in
Diagram 5d.

Diagram 6

SUPERING AND BROODCHAMBER REVERSAL

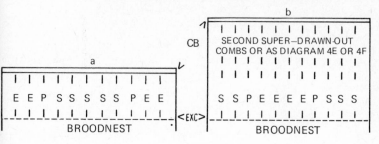

a

| | | | | | | | | | | | |
E E P S S S S P E E
BROODNEST

b

CB
SECOND SUPER—DRAWN-OUT
COMBS OR AS DIAGRAM 4E OR 4F

S S P E E E E P S S
<EXC>
BROODNEST

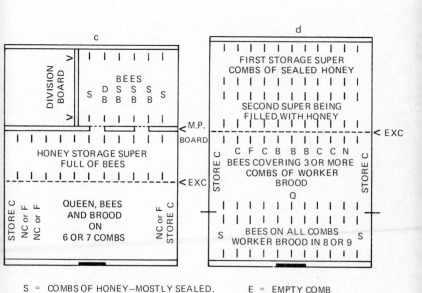

c

DIVISION BOARD

BEES
S D S S S S
B B B B
S

HONEY STORAGE SUPER
FULL OF BEES
<M.P. BOARD

<EXC

STORE C
NC or F
NC or F

QUEEN, BEES
AND BROOD
ON
6 OR 7 COMBS

NC or F
STORE C

d

FIRST STORAGE SUPER
COMBS OF SEALED HONEY

SECOND SUPER BEING
FILLED WITH HONEY

<EXC

STORE C

C F C B B B C C N
BEES COVERING 3 OR MORE
COMBS OF WORKER
BROOD

STORE C

Q

S
BEES ON ALL COMBS
WORKER BROOD IN 8 OR 9
S

S = COMBS OF HONEY—MOSTLY SEALED.
P = COMBS WITH UNSEALED HONEY
F = FRAME WITH FOUNDATION

E = EMPTY COMB
NC = NEW COMB
DB = DRONE BROOD IN COMB

Table 3. FORAGERS FOR THE FLOW

In further supering, especially towards the end of the main flow, rearrange the honey-storage combs in the supers so that the upper boxes contain only the fully sealed combs of 'ripe' honey. Any supers with unsealed honey will be put next to the excluder over the broodnest. These top supers, now ready for removal, are more easily cleared of bees when the combs of honey are sealed and have fewer bees on them.

If deep combs are needed, the main summer flow is the best time in which to obtain them by using a broodchamber filled with narrow-spaced standard frames of foundation as a honey-storage super. This is best placed as the second super. The standard combs of sealed honey can be given at the end of the season to those colonies short of stores for the winter and early spring or they can be extracted and kept to replace old poor combs removed from broodchambers in the following spring.

CHOOSING A SYSTEM OF MANAGEMENT

Whatever size of hive you choose to suit the strain of bees in your district and the average seasons to be expected, spring management must ensure that the bee colony has every opportunity of full and unrestricted growth in spring.

Table 3 shows graphically how viable eggs laid by the queen in late April, through May and into the first weeks of June become the increasing force of foraging bees needed in mid-June and through July for harvesting available nectar and converting it to honey. For example, if a queen was unable to lay eggs in both sides of one standard comb in the broodnest in one week in mid-May, this could mean the loss of 4,000 foraging bees for twenty-five to thirty days during the summer.

To minimize the incidence of swarming later on, colonies must always have at least as much hive space (in broodnest and honey-storage supers) as their adult bees can occupy without any overcrowding.

If the aim of the beekeeper is to achieve a maximum of honey production by his colony, then any method of summer management used must ensure that the whole foraging force of bees and replacements is kept healthy and 'contentedly' working as a single unit on the original site during the main nectar flow. Three points must be kept in mind and efficiently dealt with during summer management: avoidance of overcrowding; control of swarming; and rearing of replacement queens. Each of these is fully dealt with later in this chapter. They are the main problems which have always confronted beekeepers and many and varied are the methods used as solutions.

The second and third points are of paramount importance. The first is usually a contributory cause of swarming while the third is necessary for its effective control. Queen-rearing is also necessary for making increase, and by selective breeding leads to the improvement of the strain of honeybee.

SWARMING

The incidence of natural swarming in a honeybee colony — the signs and symptoms preceding it and the essential part it plays in the propagation of bee life — needs to be understood before using any method of control. Swarming is nature's method of reproduction of the honeybee colony as a complete unit.

Swarming, or the natural division of a single colony into two (or more) parts — one the prime swarm usually with the original queen and others, the parent colony left behind and possibly second swarms (each with replacement queens) — enables bee colonies to populate or colonize other areas. Without this ability to divide by swarming, natural colonies would remain located in one place, and could not increase or make up losses caused by death through starvation or disease.

Not all colonies swarm every year. Some strains are more prone to swarming than others. In a normal season in a well-managed apiary the average number of colonies making preparations for swarming is about one in three. Apart from overcrowding, the main contributory cause of swarming is the queen. If she is old and failing or otherwise unable to provide enough queen substance to inhibit the production of queen cells, the presence of these will be the usual sign that the colony, if not prevented, will swarm.

From mid-May to the end of July periodic inspections (every eight to ten days) of the broodnest of a colony may reveal the presence of many queen cells often at various stages of development. (Diagram 1a.) Unless some overriding colony behaviour causes the bees to give up the swarming preparations and break down the queen cells, the colony will swarm very soon after one of the queen cells is sealed. Swarming preparations are sometimes abandoned by the colony if most of the flying bees are diverted to a sudden copious nectar flow in good weather before the queen cells are sealed. The presence of eggs or young larvae in queen·cups is not to be regarded as a sure sign that swarming will inevitably occur. The actual issue of the swarm may be delayed for a few days by poor weather conditions and the young replacement queen(s) ready to emerge may be kept imprisoned in the cells and fed by nurse bees through small holes made in the cell caps.

Then, one day, often between 10 a.m. and 4 p.m., the colony will erupt. Literally in a few minutes from being normal in appearance with foraging bees going in and out, the entrance will be full of a struggling mass of hurrying bees, taking off in flight to become a whirling noisy swarm. These flying bees, often half the hive population, are of all ages and have filled their honeysacs before emerging. The original queen, made slim and light enough to be able to fly by having had her egg-laying curtailed some days previously, joins the swarming throng. The bees usually start forming a tight cluster on some tree branch or post not far away. Sometimes the most inaccessible spot is chosen. If the queen could not,

Photograph 4 A swarm cluster.

or did not, join the swarm cluster, the bees would soon drift back to their hive and probably issue again later on.

With the queen in the swarm cluster, scout bees — often seen making a directional guidance dance on the outside of the cluster — will have previously found a new site for the establishment of a new home.

During the time that a swarm remains in a tight cluster, the beekeeper has the opportunity of 'taking' them. By coaxing, or shaking, he gets them into an empty skep or box which they then regard as a temporary home. If he is not aware of the swarm or is unsuccessful in taking it, then suddenly all the bees and their queen will fly off to the new home. This may be some miles distant in a wall cavity, hollow tree or old derelict hive.

After the swarm has issued, clustered and departed, several happenings may be taking place in the parent colony left behind on the original site.

When bad weather has delayed the issue of the prime swarm some of the sealed queen cells may contain young virgin queens ready to emerge. When this occurs 'piping' by these young queens can often be heard in the evening if one listens near the hive. It is a clear sign that a swarm or cast will soon issue — next day if the weather is good. This high-pitched 'peep-peep' sound may be a note of fear or of challenge. It certainly causes excitement in the colony. When the prime swarm has gone and two or more of these young queens become free in the hive a fight to the death often takes place when they meet or find each other. This occurrence has been recorded on sound film. Usually, however the first young queen to emerge from a queen cell (or the survivor of a fight) will attack the immature queens in the other queen cells and kill them by stinging. Worker bees may even help in the destruction by pulling the cells apart. With only one young queen left and no queen cells, there is no further swarming.

In a colony still left populous after a prime swarm has gone from it a different happening may take place. Two young queens, free in the hive, may be kept apart by worker bees, or the imprisoned queens in the queen cells may be guarded by

Photograph 5 Part of a broodcomb showing sealed worker and drone brood and natural 'swarm' queen cells.

worker bees against the attacks of the first free virgin. Piping is again often heard. In such a case, after a few days, the free young queen, unmated, will go out with a second swarm. This is called a cast. The cast seldom settles as a cluster on a convenient tree branch and, if it does, then it only remains for a very brief time before final departure. This happening should not be confused with a mating swarm.

Such a second swarm so depletes the parent colony of its remaining adult flying bees that the one virgin queen left behind in the broodnest is allowed to destroy any remaining queen cells and become sole successor.

Yet again, in the hustle and excitement within the colony just prior to the exit of a cast, several young queens may escape from their guarded cells and go out and join the clustering bees — or even lead out much smaller casts.

The beekeeper must always try to avoid having such useless depletions of the foraging force of the colony. When a prime swarm has issued and been safely secured in a skep, his first problem is to find the hive from which it came, go through the broodnest, account for any recently vacated queen cells and make certain that only one virgin queen (or queen cell) is left.

In the natural course of events this young queen left in the parent colony will make orientation flights in two or three days. Usually within two weeks she has had her mating flight(s) and comes back to the colony to become the egg-laying mother queen.

Unless mating occurs within about thirty days, the young queen becomes incapable of mating and is only able to lay the 'unimpregnated' eggs which produce drones. She is then a useless *'drone-layer'*.

I recall one occasion at a Beekeeping Weekend School when on the Saturday afternoon I was to demonstrate 'Dealing with a colony about to swarm'. It rained and the demonstration was postponed to the Sunday morning. At 10 a.m. in good weather the colony swarmed; the swarm was safely taken in a skep and the parent colony examined. Seven queen cells with caps hanging down or off showed the recent emergence of seven virgins. Two were found dead on the floorboard, five picked off combs and put into matchboxes, and from four 'ripe' queen cells handed round to members of the audience to hold, virgins emerged within a few minutes. *All* other queen cells were destroyed and one virgin was replaced in the colony and so casting was prevented. To complete the operation: in the early evening the large swarm was housed by direct method in a new broodchamber on the original hive site, the supers of bees and honey were put on top over an excluder and the parent colony with its young queen moved several feet to one side with its entrance at right angles to the original one. The demonstration had changed to 'Dealing with a colony that has swarmed'.

Mating of a Queen Honeybee. On her mating flight(s), as

was said earlier, the young queen usually mates with several drones, sometimes on a single flight, more often on successive flights. This may mean that the total male sperm kept alive for several years in her sperm sac may be from drones of a different strain or even race — at the best (for bee-breeding) from brother drones.

In bee-breeding this is one of the great difficulties that has to be faced when attempting to maintain a good strain of honeybee by careful selection. In most other forms of live-stock single mating between selected male and female parents can be controlled and enables the breeder to select the desirable characteristics in each, prior to mating, and by line-breeding establish these good points in their offspring.

Young Queens and Swarming. Once the young queen starts laying normal worker brood in the colony, it is most exceptional for her to go out with a swarm in that same season. Indeed, if she is well mated, healthy and of good strain, the colony she heads during her first full season, in the next year, seldom shows signs of swarming if properly housed and well managed. Many independent records show that the incidence of swarming in colonies headed by such good young queens in their first year is less than one in twenty. This may be due to her ability to provide sufficient queen substance to inhibit queen cell formation by the worker bees and keep the colony welded together as a single unit.

Hunger Swarms can occur when a colony facing starvation leaves the hive in search of another home in a last effort to survive.

Forced Swarms usually result from serious overcrowding.

Mating Swarms are usually a case of bees leaving a small poorly provisioned nucleus hive at the same time as a queen goes out to mate. The bees do not accompany her to her mating and often return after she has been mated or settle somewhere as a small cast.

Absconding Swarms can happen when a 'taken' swarm is without its queen or a hived swarm dislikes its new home.

SUPERSEDURE

From the foregoing description of natural swarming and the subsequent requeening of the parent colony, it would appear that this is the only way in which colonies replace their queens. This is not so, since many old or failing queens are superseded by young ones, without swarming, although a few queen cells are present in the colony. In most cases of supersedure, only one or two queen cells are made by the worker bees and these cells are usually constructed over a hatching egg or very young larva in a worker cell — not a queen cup. The cell mouth is enlarged and so the base of a supersedure cell will start at the mid-rib of the comb, and not from the face of the comb as is usual in swarm cells. Supersedure cells are usually found towards the end of the summer when swarming-time has passed. For some weeks the old queen may have laid only a few hundreds of eggs (or less) in scattered patches. The combs of her brood show a pepperbox appearance where non-viable eggs have failed to hatch out. The old queen may still be engaged in this sort of egg-laying while the young daughter queen mates, returns to the colony and starts laying. Many cases are on record where an old marked queen and her daughter have been observed in the same broodnest, and sometimes actually laying eggs on the same broodcomb. By the autumn the old queen has usually disappeared. A few strains of honeybee show a proneness to replacing the old queen by supersedure instead of swarming.

Provided the supersedure takes place while the colony is still strong and in good health — and the old queen has previously headed a worthwhile colony for two seasons — then the supersedure is valuable to the beekeeper. What is a worthwhile colony? One that was good-tempered, had not swarmed and had produced an above average surplus of honey each season would be well worth while.

Whenever eggs and young brood with worker bees become separated from the queen and the remainder of the colony by a substantial barrier — such as combs of honey in supers, or an excluder or a screen board — queen cells are likely to be formed and queens raised by the worker bees. The likelihood

57

is dependent on the remoteness and completeness of the separation of the two portions. Such a colony is clearly not queenless nor the queen old or failing. The lack of easy continued contact with the queen-right part of the colony may have deprived the bees covering the young brood in the separated part from receiving, through food-sharing, their 'daily ration' of queen substance needed to inhibit queen cell formation. The bees in this remote part may then consider themselves to be queenless and the queen cells are raised under a supersedure or emergency impulse. The method will be described in chapter 7.

Marking queens. When describing supersedure, I referred to a 'marked queen'. The general behaviour of a queen bee on the comb, her slower movements, and the worn fringe of hairs on the front of her thorax and on the segments of her abdomen may be a guide to her age, but only some definite method of marking can provide immediate and accurate information. A marked queen is far easier to find when the need arises. Some experienced beekeepers with a large number of colonies in out-apiaries identify queens by clipping the wings. A queen with clipped wings cannot fly far or high and if a swarm should occur then the cluster will be low down and near the hive. With the beekeeper carrying out routine visits to his apiaries every eight to ten days, the swarms, if they happen, are usually easily seen and secured and are not lost.

Clipping the queen bee's wings does not cause pain or lead to her being considered 'failing' by the bees and seldom causes subsequent supersedure. The broad third of the wings cut off are as nerveless as our own fingernails. The clipping of wings is a delicate and precise operation to carry out. It is wise to practise on expendable drones and become efficient before attempting the operation on a valuable queen.

Another method of marking queens is by a bright-coloured spot on the upper surface of her thorax. The use of a different colour each year indicates her age. She is always very easily seen in the broodnest. Such a mark does not prevent her normal flight with a swarm. A quick-drying 'dope' (as used for model aircraft) or nail varnish is quite suitable for making the mark with a fine brush or the butt end of a matchstick.

Bee-appliance dealers can supply a kit for queen-marking. This includes a small and convenient press in cage to put over the queen on the comb and hold her still, without damage. Using this cage the operation is easier — but again practise first on drones or worker bees.

SWARM PREVENTION AND CONTROL

In the main, prevention is achieved by the good spring management of all colonies (chapter 4), and the use of a system of swarm control which includes the requeening of at least half of the colonies each year with young tested queens of good strain.

'Cull the worst and breed from the best' is a very sound maxim to follow with honeybees as with any other livestock. By keeping records of bee colonies — their honey surplus, hardiness, economy in wintering, disease resistance, lack of proneness to swarm, temper, and the suitability of the strain for the district and size of broodnest used — one or more colonies can be chosen as breeders of future queens. Others will show which queens need early replacement. All too often poor colonies are allowed to replace their queens with little hope of any improvement simply because it was the easiest thing to do at the moment.

No apiary need house colonies which are virtually ill-tempered, non-paying guests. Drones from such undesirable colonies are a menace to any plans for upgrading the strain of bee in the apiary.

Using natural swarms. Control of swarming presupposes the need for control. Some beekeeepers with near-by apiaries are able to keep a constant watch during the critical swarming period. They allow nature to take its course and rely upon securing any swarms that issue. The swarmed colony is dealt with as previously described.

1. If neither increase nor requeening from this strain are wanted, then next day destroy *all* queen cells and any free virgins in this parent broodnest. Eight or nine days later, 59

Diagram 7   MULTIPURPOSE BOARD $\left(\begin{smallmatrix}\text{SIZE TO SUIT}\\\text{HIVE IN USE}\end{smallmatrix}\right)$

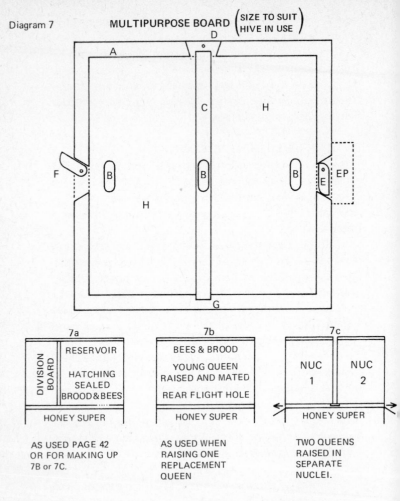

7a	7b	7c
DIVISION BOARD RESERVOIR / HATCHING SEALED BROOD & BEES	BEES & BROOD / YOUNG QUEEN RAISED AND MATED / REAR FLIGHT HOLE	NUC 1 / NUC 2
HONEY SUPER	HONEY SUPER	HONEY SUPER
AS USED PAGE 42 OR FOR MAKING UP 7B or 7C.	AS USED WHEN RAISING ONE REPLACEMENT QUEEN	TWO QUEENS RAISED IN SEPARATE NUCLEI.

MP BOARD. (AUTHOR'S ADAPTION) FOR USE AS COVER, CLEARER OR SCREENBOARD.

A. FRAMING STRIPS, $1\frac{1}{4}$" WIDE, TO PROVIDE A BEESPACE ($\frac{1}{4}$"–$\frac{5}{16}$") ON BOTH SIDES.

B. BEE ESCAPE' HOLES.

C. CENTRE STRIP ($1\frac{1}{2}$" WIDE), THICKNESS SAME AS TOP FRAMING.

D. REAR ENTRANCE WEDGE (5"), SLOTTED TO RECEIVE CENTRE STRIP.

E. F. SIDE ENTRANCE WEDGES (5"), MADE TO HINGE OPEN, IN TOP FRAMING ONLY.

G. SLOT IN FRONT TOP FRAMING, TO HOLD CENTRE STRIP.

H. SHEET OF RESIN BONDED PLYWOOD AT LEAST 5mm THICK.

EP. ENTRANCE ALIGHTING PLATFORM.

"BEE ESCAPES", SEVERAL PIECES (5" x 3") OF PERFORATED ZINC AND EXCLUDER NEEDED IN/OVER HOLES AS ALTERNATIVE USAGE DEMANDS.

when the bees are flying well, move it to the other side of the old site with its entrance again pointing away from the original one. Carry out a second destruction of queen cells. The swarm, now settled down, will be reinforced by the flying bees of the parent broodnest. When they come back from foraging these bees will go into the nearest colony (that is, the swarm) since their own has gone.

In three or four days the parent broodnest with its remaining bees and sealed brood can be safely united to the swarm by putting the broodchamber over an excluder, or on top of an MP board (with excluder over the holes) over the supers or the uniting can be done by using the newspaper method (see page 86). When all the worker brood has emerged any bees still on the combs can be shaken on to a board in front of the entrance and the combs used elsewhere. If shaking off the bees is not desired they can be cleared by putting a clearer board with bee escapes fitted under the brood chamber. If an MP board was used it would simply mean replacing the pieces of excluder with bee escapes.

With this method no increase is made from the progeny of this 'swarm' queen, and the maximum of foragers have been available for the flow. At the end of the season this old unwanted queen must be replaced by a strain-bred tested young queen so that it will winter with every prospect of being an even better colony next season.

2. There is another successful variation which provides for the raising of a strain-bred tested young queen for the replacement needed at the end of the season. After the second destruction of queen cells described above, a 'ripe' strain-bred queen cell (from a queen-rearing unit) can be given to the sealed brood and bees left in the brood-chamber. This unit must remain on its location and will need feeding. When you are using single-walled hives, the broodchamber with bees and brood in it can be placed on top of the 'swarm' hive after the second destruction of queen cells, over an MP board. In the MP board the bee-escape holes must be covered with a piece of glass or thin wood, or with perforated zinc on both upper and lower sides of the holes. This is to prevent any

61

contact, even by tongues, between bees in the upper box and the colony below. This done, a 'ripe' selected queen cell can be given, by carefully pressing it into a thumb impression made near the top of a comb containing sealed brood. Feeding will be needed and is best done by using an internal frame feeder. The rear entrance should be opened at dusk the same evening. (Diagram 7b.)

If there were plenty of bees and sealed brood left after the second queen cell destruction, it would be possible to make up two separate four-comb nuclei, each with frame feeder and provided with a selected queen cell. In this case the MP board would have its central division strip in position and the side entrances opened later in the evening. (Diagram 7c.)

The beekeeper, especially the beginner, may not have the essential item for success — a 'ripe' selected strain-bred queen cell. Even this difficulty can be overcome. A 'prepared' comb (see chapter 7) of eggs and very young brood can previously be taken from the broodnest of a breeder queen where it was placed some five or six days before. The bees are brushed off the comb when it is taken out and the comb kept warm to prevent any chilling of the brood and eggs. This comb is placed in the centre of the brood and bees in the parent broodnest after the second destruction of its queen cells. In seven or eight days there will be queen cells to select from, and they can then be carefully cut out and used, or reduced to one if only a single replacement queen is needed.

If none of these improvements of strain are possible, then you will have to *leave* one good, well-placed queen cell when you carry out the second destruction of the queen cells in the parent broodnest. Do not at any time shake a comb on which there is a queen cell you wish to use.

3.   If, however, the queen with the swarm had been in her second full season and records of the colony she had headed were satisfactory, the beekeeper may want to take this opportunity of making increase, or at least of raising a replacement queen. To do this, the queen cells in the parent hive are not destroyed the day after the swarm has been hived. Dependent on the amount of increase wanted, one queen cell, preferably

unsealed, can be left in the broodnest to produce the replacement queen, or two or three nuclei can be made up each with a comb having a selected queen cell on it. Relying on having a single queen successfully mated is a risk. She may get lost at mating. The best solution is to make up a four-comb nucleus with a good queen cell, give it a frame feeder and, if it is to remain in the apiary as a separate unit, lightly plug up the small entrance with dry grass until the next day. The remaining combs and bees in the parent broodnest are gently pushed to one side and flanked by a division board. Only one selected queen cell will have been left. This unit will also need feeding. In both units the bees may attempt and succeed in raising more queen cells so an inspection must be made in five or six days, when any further queen cells must be destroyed. A drawing-pin previously put on the top bar will show which was the selected queen cell — which by this time may have been vacated by the virgin queen. Carry out this inspection very carefully, use very little smoke and use covercloths. Virgin queens are easily alarmed and are good flyers. If they should fly off, just leave the combs as they were, stand still and wait. They usually come back.

Using MP boards as described in (2) above, the nucleus colony could be put on another hive while the broodchamber could go on top of the swarm over an MP board. In both cases open the entrance wedges in the evening of the next day. These various ways of dealing with the queen cells and the parent broodnest are all proved and successful methods, provided always that the prime swarm has been secured and not lost. The risk of losing an unobserved swarm makes it an uncertain system for 'weekend' beekeepers or those with out-apiaries.

Positive swarm control. Control of swarming before the swarm issues must involve a routine inspection of all colonies in order to ascertain if swarming preparations are taking place. These inspections are usually only needed during the critical period from late May to the end of July. Diagnosis of the condition of the broodnest during such an inspection involves taking note of the proportions of brood (sealed,

63

unsealed, eggs) in the broodnest, the age of the queen, presence of drones, the amount of room left for expansion and any swarm preparations. This diagnosis taken in conjunction with the weather prospects and the state of the nectar flow enables skilled beekeepers to decide how many days can safely be left before making the next inspection and what should be done at the time to induce the colony to give up any early swarming preparations.

1.   During the *first* inspection, if occupied queen cells are found, destroy *all* of them. The examination of the broodnest must be thorough, no queen cell must be overlooked. Take particular care when inspecting the edges and bottom of all combs. If the queen was still in 'full lay' and the broodcombs contained large patches of eggs and very young larvae then queen cells are unlikely to be found, but if there were few eggs and only a little open brood and a large amount of sealed brood then the finding of queen cells is more likely. Where only unsealed queen cells have been found and destroyed or where diagnosis shows some relief in the broodnest is needed, carry out the necessary manipulation and operation before closing the broodnest.

In some colonies the removal of a few combs of sealed brood and stores from the broodnest to a reservoir (Diagram 7a) on top of an MP board on another hive and the replacement of them with empty combs or frames of foundation can well provide work for idle wax-secreting bees and later more young brood for nurse bees to supply with bee milk. In other colonies the addition of another honey super, or the moving of one already partly drawn out, next to the broodchamber, will be all that is considered necessary. Diagnosis of the broodnest will have shown what was needed and by providing it then and there the colony can be kept in a balanced condition.

Make a note on a record card or in a book that a further examination will be needed — in seven or more days, according to the diagnosis. The next routine inspection will show that in many colonies, especially those with strain-bred young queens in their first season, restoring the balance in the colony was all that was needed to prevent any further preparations for swarming.

Through lack of forethought or lack of equipment, this routine cutting-out or destruction of queen cells too often becomes the sole continuous weekly treatment. It is a frustration method of control and is only mentioned to be condemned. Sooner or later the bees become thwarted and during one of the weekly destructions, when the bees are testy, a small scrub queen cell, only capable of producing a poorly nourished ill-formed useless young semi-queen, will be overlooked, or missed. This will be enough to cause the issue of an unobserved and probably lost swarm. Even if swarming was prevented, the colony is finally left with its old queen whose failure to satisfy the colony might well have been the reason for the swarming preparations.

2. At the second inspection, if more queen cells have been built and particularly if at the first inspection some of the destroyed queen cells were sealed, then a positive method of swarm control involving *dequeening* is recommended.

With all the necessary equipment to hand and when this second inspection has shown more queen cells, first find the queen and put her on her comb — no queen cell must be left on it — into a separate nucleus hive, add two more combs of bees and brood, shake in the bees from another comb and add a store comb. There must be no queen cells on any of these combs. Cover the nucleus and block up the entrance lightly with a plug of grass or a piece of perforated zinc until next day. Move it to one side, several feet away and with entrance at right angles to the parent hive.

Destroy, by pinching out, *all* queen cells left on any comb in the original broodnest. Move them together to one side of the broodchamber and add the necessary four combs/frames of foundation to replace those used in the nucleus.

The colony will now be queenless and will build emergency queen cells round some of the eggs or young larvae.

Using single-walled hives and an MP board, the nucleus with the queen could be placed on top of the MP board which must have all the bee-escape holes completely covered, and the entrance wedge opened next day. It will need feeding. As you will have to inspect this same colony again it is more convenient to put the nucleus with the queen on top of the MP board on a similar adjacent hive. It is most unlikely that any further queen cells will be made in it but a check next time will make sure.

You will finish by having removed the queens from all those colonies which had produced further queen cells. No swarms can occur and the colonies will go on storing honey.

In Britain it is very unusual for queen cells to be constructed before the beginning of June in the broodnest of a colony which has had good spring management and adequate room for expansion. The exception is where colonies are located in a fruit blossom area which provides an early main flow. This will be dealt with later. Any eggs laid by the queen after the beginning of June will not produce bees of an age to be of value in the main summer flow (see Table 3). The first destruction of queen cells and the provision of relief can further extend her egg-laying. Her removal at the second inspection, probably in mid-June, when queen cells are again found, does not therefore in itself affect the number of foragers for the main nectar flow.

In actual fact it increases their potential. After the removal of the queen there will be no young brood to nurse and feed for two or three weeks. When young nurse bees are relieved of heavy nursing duties and consequently do not use up their glandular reserves, they have an increased length of adult life due to their better physiological condition. They can be foraging bees for six or seven weeks instead of about four.

Before the next visit a *decision,* based on the recorded diagnosis of each dequeened colony, must be made. Do you want to and are you able to improve the strain of honeybee when you make provision for the requeening of the colony? Will you have a young strain-bred queen or selected queen cell to use? If not, you will have to requeen from the progeny of the original queen, whether her worker bees were bad tempered, prone to swarming or poor honey-getters.

The art and craft of successful beekeeping depends upon the ability to do the right operations at the correct time.

3. Nine or ten days later — it must not be under nine or over ten if the plan decided upon is to be completed in one single operation — a third visit is necessary. The alternative plans that could then be used are:

Plan A: All the emergency queen cells are destroyed and a selected strain-bred queen cell is given. (Photographs 8—10.)

Plan B: All the emergency queen cells are destroyed and a young strain-bred mated and laying queen is introduced by herself in a wire-mesh cage (see page 85).

Plan C: All the emergency queen cells are destroyed and a three- or four-comb nucleus with the young laying queen is united to the parent broodnest by using the newspaper method (see Diagrams 9a and 9b).

Plan D: All the emergency queen cells are destroyed and a prepared comb of eggs and very young larvae from a breeder queen is placed between two combs of sealed brood in the broodnest. Seven days later, one unsealed queen cell on this comb is left, all others being destroyed.

Plan E: Leave one of the emergency queen cells, preferably one which is unsealed, of good shape, position and well provided with food, and destroy all other queen cells.

Plan F: Destroy all emergency queen cells and replace the old queen and her nucleus using the newspaper method of uniting. (Diagrams 9a and 9b.) This last plan is best kept as a reserve solution to the problem of requeening when, after about two weeks, an inspection showed that any of the other plans had proved unsuccessful and there was no young queen starting to lay 'worker' eggs in the colony.

My own order of preference would be plans C, B, A, D, E — and F. The timing of this operation to be done in nine or ten days after the removal of the queen is to ensure that when the emergency queen cells are destroyed there will be no brood left that is young enough for the bees to use to make any more queen cells.

If visits and operations are rigidly restricted to weekends, that is, every seven days, then on the first visit seven days after the removal of the old queen, in all plans except E (where one unsealed cell is left), destroy all the emergency queen cells. At the same time either of plans A or E can be followed. On the next visit a check must be made for any more emergency queen cells.

Plans B, C and D are best left to the second of the seven-. day or weekend visits when again any further emergency queen cells will be destroyed before carrying out the chosen plan.

Positive swarm control plans for special districts and flows. When it is wished to move colonies of bees to a heather district early in August then any of the above plans for swarm control, in which a new young tested queen is laying her worker eggs in the broodnest during mid-June and through July, is very suitable. Table 3 shows that such eggs will produce the foraging force of bees needed at the time heather is in flower. When working for section honey, put on a crate (or rack) of sections before the end of the summer flow so that the wax foundation in them can be partly drawn out into honeycomb. When preparing the colony for going to the heather, rearrange the broodnest to enable the queen to continue laying and also to encourage the bees to put the honey in the sections rather than in the broodnest. Diagram 8a shows the type of rearrangement that is recommended. Incoming nectar from the heather cannot be stored in the outer combs for a fortnight or more because of the brood in them. As the bees emerge from the central combs of sealed brood, the young queen will lay eggs in the vacated worker cells and so these central combs will in turn not be used for honey storage for three weeks. When the colony is brought back to the apiary, these central combs will provide some empty cell space for the bees to cluster in and on during the winter.

In districts where there is a main flow from fruit blossom (particularly cherry and plum) or when colonies of bees are taken to such areas for pollination purposes, the queen usually reaches her peak of egg-laying several weeks before those in other areas. In such cases a method of *artificial*

Diagram 8

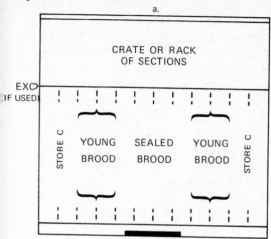

a.

CRATE OR RACK
OF SECTIONS

EXC>
IF USED

| STORE C | YOUNG BROOD | SEALED BROOD | YOUNG BROOD | STORE C |

BROODNEST AS REARRANGED FOR HEATHER FLOW

b.

PREPARED COMB SHOWING
LINE OF CUT TO EXPOSE
EGGS AND YOUNG LARVAE

DISCARDED PORTION

LARVA–12 to 24 HOURS OLD

PREPARED COMB FOR QUEEN REARING

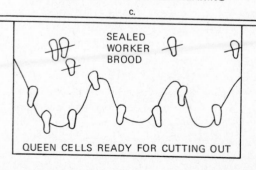

c.

SEALED
WORKER
BROOD

QUEEN CELLS READY FOR CUTTING OUT

QUEEN CELL CUT OUT
WITH HEEL

swarming can be carried out early in May and is best done before any queen cells are started. Following the routine inspection technique already described and using cross-fire smoking, put the supers of honey on a flat roof. Move the broodchamber with the queen and bees from its floor on to another flat roof table. Put an empty broodchamber on the floorboard. Using covercloths, find the queen and put her on her comb into the middle of this new broodchamber. Fill it up with its complement of drawn-out empty combs and some frames of foundation. The excluder is placed over this broodchamber and the supers are restored. The crownboard on top of the supers is replaced by an MP board with the bee-escape holes completely covered; its rear-entrance wedge should be opened later — that evening if possible. On top of this MP board place the original brood-chamber, after pushing the combs together and adding a spare comb on one flank. The ordinary-crownboard, which was on the supers, shaken free of bees, is placed on top of this upper broodchamber and the roof replaced.

Five days later, inspect the broodcombs in this top broodchamber and remove any *sealed* queen cells, since these will have been constructed over larvae too old to receive full nutrition as a queen. Nine or ten days later go through the combs again and either leave one selected queen cell to provide a replacement queen or make up two or three nuclei each with a good queen cell. The bees and brood in this top broodchamber will have needed feeding from the start.

The young queens should be mated and laying well when the main clover flow commences. The broodchamber with the young queen can be united to the colony after the removal of the broodchamber with the old queen.

The broodchamber with this old queen and combs of bees and brood is put on top of the hive above the MP board. The queen can be killed and her brood allowed to hatch out, after being checked for emergency queen cells, and when the coverings of the bee-escape holes on the MP board are replaced with pieces of excluder, the bees will join those below. No entrance is open in the MP board.

If you wished, after killing the queen, you could allow the brood and bees to raise emergency queen cells, one of which would be selected as before. In this case the bee-escape holes would be covered and a rear entrance given.

Artificial swarming as described — or one of its tested and proved variations — has always been a most successful method of swarm control. It is best carried out before queen cells are found, but very often succeeds if the queen cells are all unsealed. When sealed queen cells are present it is less reliable because the swarming impulse in the colony has become too fixed to alter.

In this chapter it has been assumed throughout that the broodnest is in a single standard broodchamber. In very many cases it will have been in two broodchambers, either a standard broodchamber and a shallow super-box as an extension or two standard broodchambers.

What should you do with the shallow extension or the additional broodchamber when carrying out the swarm control operations as described?

At the first destruction of queen cells as described in Positive Swarm Control operation 1, put another excluder between the two boxes in the following way:

Remove the roof and place the honey supers on it. On another roof table put the shallow extension or second broodchamber, covered with a covercloth. Go through the bottom broodchamber, still on its floorboard, and destroy all queen cells found in it. If the queen is seen, make certain she remains in this bottom box. When all queen cells, if found, are destroyed put on the excluder and cover it with a cloth. Now inspect the shallow extension or the other broodchamber in the same way. If the queen is found in the shallow extension then place her or coax her into the broodchamber on the floorboard. If she is found in the second broodchamber, exchange this one (after destruction of queen cells) with the one on the floorboard. If you cannot find her then shake off all the bees from the combs, and any left on the sides of the box, on to a board placed in front of the hive entrance. A suitable empty box in which to place the shaken combs makes the operation easier. Keep it covered as each empty comb is added to it.

The queen must now be in the bottom broodchamber. Put the extension or queenless broodchamber (no queen cells left in either) on top of the excluder covering the bottom broodchamber. Put the original excluder on top of it and restore the supers and roof.

If no queen cells were found, the broodnest would be restored as it was before commencing the operation. If queen cells are found at a later inspection then the same routine should be followed.

At Positive Swarm Control operation 2, before dequeening destroy all queen cells in this upper box that was between the two excluders. Keep it covered with a cloth. When reassembling the hive after dequeening and completion of operation 2, put the super extension or the broodchamber on top of an excluder over the supers. The arrangement of the hive will now be: floorboard, broodchamber without the queen, excluder, supers, excluder, box of emerging brood, crownboard, roof.

At operation 3 nine or ten days later, first inspect this top box and remove all queen cells. When reassembling the hive after completing the operation, the excluder under this top box can be removed. Any sealed brood in the combs will emerge and join the colony. Some honey will be stored in this upper box and at the end of the season when a young queen is laying worker brood in the bottom broodchamber, the super extension or second broodchamber can be put back over the queen-right broodnest — without an excluder in between.

This is a very good way of ensuring ample stores of honey for the wintering of the bee colony and usually obviates the need for autumn feeding with sugar syrup.

CHAPTER 7
Queen-Rearing, Queen-Introduction, Uniting

The rearing of queen honeybees for replacing old, failing or undesirable queens in the colonies in the apiary is an essential part of good beekeeping. It is also necessary when increase in the number of colonies is wanted.

In small apiaries with perhaps only three or four colonies the use of natural queen cells from the best colonies will satisfy the beekeeper's requirements. The various ways in which this can be done have already been described in chapter 6.

The term 'strain-bred' has been applied to selected queen cells and young queens. This term implies that wherever possible only those queen cells raised by a selected colony should be used to provide young replacement queens. On what basis is a colony selected? In addition to those listed earlier some further qualities merit consideration. With normal good management, the chosen colony would have gone through the previous season without any necessity for swarm control, and have yielded a higher-than-average surplus of honey. These two factors indicate that the strain of bee was suited to the size of broodnest used, the district and system of management. They also show that the queen was able to keep the colony welded together as a single industrious unit. Was the colony economical in the use of winter stores? In the spring, was it strong in bees and brood and showed no signs of dysentery? If so, this shows good health and vitality. During manipulations were the bees quiet on the combs and not given to stinging? This shows good temper — but do not attribute bad temper to the bees if the manipulations were clumsy or carried out in poor weather conditions.

A colony with such a good record can justly be regarded as a useful 'breeder'.

Unfortunately, in Britain, the queen heading this good colony is almost certain to be a mongrel and so you cannot hope to breed true from her or hope to retain all her good points in all her progeny, especially when they will be mated with several different drones.

These difficulties should not daunt any beekeeper from doing what he can in his own apiary, however small it may be. By his keeping records and using only those queen cells produced by his best colonies and by encouraging his beekeeping neighbours to do likewise, the general quality of bee stock must improve.

In apiaries with six to ten colonies there may be three that could be used as breeders. Look at the bees in the three colonies in early May when drones first appear and have not had time to drift in from other colonies. The marking of some of the bees will show more signs of mongrelism than others. Of the three colonies – other factors being equal – choose the one where the worker bees are all of the same appearance in body colour and markings and where the drones of the colony show no variations in the colour of the segments of the abdomen. My own preference would be to choose those that were uniformly dark and not banded in any way.

An egg from a breeder queen will have started as a single cell in her ovaries, and in the chromosomes in the nucleus of the egg cell there will be only the one set of hereditary factors which resulted from the union of the queen's mother and one of her drone mates. If this egg is not impregnated with sperm from one of her own drone mates, then, as stated earlier, it can only produce a drone. The drone, therefore, has no father and inherits and transmits only the one set of hereditary characters derived from his grandparents, through his mother. This form of virgin birth or reproduction without mating is termed parthenogenesis.

If the egg is impregnated with sperm before it is laid by the queen then the chromosomes in the single fertilized egg cell will be a mixture of two sets of hereditary characteristics. One set will be from the queen mother and the other set from the sperm of one of her drone mates. This mixture is not necessarily in half-and-half proportions because in this fertilized egg a random assortment of the genes in the chromosomes takes place in a series of changes known biologically as meiosis. This happens before the embryo in the egg cell starts its development. This type of egg will produce a female bee, which can become a worker bee or a queen bee according to the type of cell in which it develops and the different form of nutrition it is given. The hereditary factors are exactly the same at the start but from an early stage (after about thirty-six hours) differential feeding is responsible for the progressive changes necessary to make either a worker or a queen.

In queen-rearing, to ensure that the queen cells are well nourished and nurtured, they must be raised in a populous colony well provided with young bees, ample food and free from any disease.

PLANNED QUEEN-REARING

Most methods of queen-rearing depend on the fact that when a queen is removed, the colony will, in an effort to survive, raise replacement queens by giving very young chosen larvae the different nutritional feeding in the kind of cell needed for the raising of a young queen. By knowing how long each stage in the development process takes, the bee-keeper is able to predict when the queen cells so raised will be available for use. To obtain the best-nurtured queens he must make certain that they were nurtured as queens from the stage when the larvae were between 12 and 24 hours old. Bees can raise semi-queens from larvae as old as 72 hours. To prevent this, the beekeeper inspects the bee colony four days after the removal of the queen and destroys any sealed queen cells that are found. They will have been made from larvae over 24 hours old and so could not have had full nurture as future queens. At the same time he will restrict the number of unsealed queen cells left to one or two more than he will eventually need. When doing this he should not choose any queen cell next to drone brood, or any twin queen cells, but well-placed, well-separated queen cells and, if possible, those made on different combs. No comb of bees must be shaken; use a feather or thin twig to brush the bees aside when inspecting the vertically held comb.

Plan A: When the broodnest of the chosen breeder queen   75 fills at least a standard broodchamber and has eight or nine combs of brood, make an artificial swarm. Choose a time when the bees are flying strongly and nectar is still being brought in. In general, this state of the colony will be reached before the end of May and without any queen cells being made. For this variation of artificial swarming another empty hive will be needed if double-walled equipment is being used. With single-walled equipment in use a spare floor, crown-board, broodchamber and roof will be required when the divided colony has to be placed on separate sites.

The basic operation entails the division of the colony into two separated units. One broodnest will have the original queen on her comb, a store comb and a comb with sealed brood, all with adhering bees. The other will have the remaining combs and most of the young brood and eggs. Spare combs or frames with foundation are used to fill up the broodnests. The hives or units will be separated with entrances at right angles. The queenless unit which will raise queen cells is best left on the original site and fed. The honey supers are restored to the queen-right unit over an excluder.

If an MP board is used with single-walled equipment the queen-right unit can remain on the original site and the queen-cell raising unit is placed over the MP board on top of the supers with one hole in the board covered with excluder and the others with glass. The rear entrance is opened the next day. This upper queenless unit should be fed.

Any broodnest extension (super-box) of the original unit can be restored in place with the queen-right unit.

Four days after making the two units completely separate, inspect the combs in the queen-rearing unit, destroy any sealed queen cells and restrict the number of unsealed queen cells, leaving only a few more than will be required. Using covercloths, expose only one comb at a time and so minimize the loss of bees.

The day before the young queens are due to emerge, make up three-comb nuclei each with a 'ripe' queen cell. Where necessary other or extra nuclei — made up two days previously by using combs of sealed brood and stores from

76

other colonies — could be given any spare queen cells.

Each mating nucleus should contain a comb of honey and pollen — if the honey was sealed then lightly bruise the cappings before it is put in — a comb of old sealed brood with no larvae or eggs in it, another comb of stores and a frame feeder of sugar syrup. All combs should be well covered with bees.

To prevent the flying bees in the nuclei from returning to the original site, the small entrances of the separate nuclei are best plugged with dry grass until the evening of the next day. Better still, take the nuclei when made up to another apiary some few miles away. If the queen cells have been placed in them they must not be jarred or the combs allowed to swing against each other during the moving and, of course, they must have no frame feeders full of syrup when being moved. Whenever transporting combs of bees, arrange that the top bars of the frames point in the direction the car is going — never across it. Put in the frame feeders after completing the journey.

Co-operation between several friendly beekeepers who have the same ideas and plans can make queen-rearing a real pleasure. They can help each other in deciding on suitable breeder colonies and arrange for one colony to be a drone-breeder. This drone-producing colony could be established in a temporary convenient out-apiary some miles from any other bees. Drone-free mating-nuclei could be taken to it and the problem of preventing the loss of flying bees from nuclei would not arise.

If the mating-nuclei have to remain in the one apiary, then some restriction of poor drones to prevent their flying at mating time is still possible. Five or six weeks before the young queens will be due to mate — that is, about eight or nine days after emergence from the queen cells — put a frame fitted with drone foundation in the colonies whose drones are considered good. Try to avoid using the colony from which the queen-raising unit, or the prepared comb, will be obtained. Late in the evening of the day after making up the nuclei with queen cells, put excluders under the broodchambers of all colonies which have undesirable drones and leave the excluders there for about two weeks.

Plan B: This involves using a prepared comb of eggs and very young larvae from the chosen breeder colony. It is a variation of the well-known 'Miller' method for raising selected queen cells. Carry out an operation similar to plan A, but with these differences: The single broodchamber left on the original site must contain only store combs and combs of fully sealed worker brood, all with the adhering bees. Not a single egg or young larva must be in any of the cells of the combs in this broodnest. This is to make certain that no queen cell could be raised from an egg or young brood of this queen and the queenless bees can only use the selected eggs and young brood in the prepared comb given some six or seven hours later. Shake in the young bees from several combs before transferring them to the queen-right unit. If two standard broodchambers were in use, there may be some combs left. These can be put in a reservoir broodchamber on another hive.

When an MP board is used, plan B is the same as plan A except that all holes in the board should be covered with perforated zinc. Whenever possible a feed of sugar syrup should be given in an internal frame feeder.

The timing of this operation is important: if the rearrangement was done in the mid-morning, the prepared comb could be given that same evening and the rear entrance opened next day.

The prepared comb is obtained by placing a frame fitted with unwired wax foundation into the broodnest of the breeder queen, next to the one in which she is laying. This is done five or six days before it is required in plan B. If you have a new empty comb previously drawn out or mostly drawn out, it can be put in four days before it is wanted.

The breeder queen will lay eggs in this comb. It is then removed from the broodnest, all the adhering bees brushed, not shaken, from it, and an empty comb is put in its place.

This comb of eggs and possibly some very young larvae can now be taken to a warm room indoors and prepared. The preparation is done to make the removal of the resulting queen cells an easy operation and to prevent too many in-different queen cells being raised. Using a sharp knife, cut the comb so that eggs or very young larvae (12 hours old) are left at the exposed edges and have a 3 in. gap below them, as in Diagram 8b. Now using a matchstick crush any eggs or larvae in three out of every four cells on both sides of the lower edge of the cut portion. The finished preparation should leave only one live larva or hatching egg with no other eggs or larvae within ½ in. of it. The lower portion of the cut comb will have been cut out, and discarded before selecting the larvae. This unwanted portion, after similar treatment, could be fastened in a frame and used as in Positive Swarm Control plan D. If the mouth of the hexagonal worker cell containing a selected egg or larva is carefully widened, and made circular, its selection as a future queen cell is improved.

The prepared comb is placed in the *centre* of the queenless unit. Remove an empty comb, shake off the bees and make the central gap for the insertion of the prepared comb. Use covercloths when doing this operation.

Four days later, take out this prepared comb and destroy any queen cells that are sealed. Most probably there are none but at the same time reduce the number of unsealed queen cells being made to the numbers required. This will concentrate the nutrition of the queen cells left. When select-ing, look in each young queen cell to see that it contains a pearly white larva resting on a bed of cream-like royal jelly and is well apart from its neighbour.

Nine or ten days later — not longer — the queen cells will be ready for distribution to mating nuclei made up two days earlier (Diagram 8 c).

Into an empty nucleus box put two combs of bees from the queen cell-raising unit, then put the comb of selected queen cells in between them for safety. Always carry it care-fully and upright as you go to each mating nucleus.

Carefully cut out one of the selected queen cells with a ½ in. 'heel' all round its base. Make a thumb impression in the comb of sealed brood in the mating nucleus and holding the

79

Photograph 6 Making a thumb impression for a selected queen cell.

Photograph 7 The selected queen cell pushed into the thumb impression.

queen cell only by the 'heel', push it firmly into the depression. See that it is secure and put the comb back very carefully. Proceed likewise with the other mating nuclei. The last queen cell can be left on the prepared comb and the three combs of the nucleus you have been carrying around given back to the queen-raising unit to provide a replacement for the old queen below.

Carried out correctly this method is most successful and is widely used when ten or twelve queen cells are needed. It is recommended for use by the more experienced beekeepers with quite large apiaries.

Later, when the young queens are mated and have been laying long enough for sealed worker brood to be seen, they can be called mated and tested young queens. When the workers emerge and a careful check shows that they are all very much like those of the breeder queen, then the young queen could be called strain-bred.

Wherever possible overwinter the chosen and used breeder queen in a strong, healthy, well-provided colony. If she has headed the colony during this second season without its swarming she is worth breeding from in the next year. She should have been marked to show her age. If in the spring at the start of her third season she still heads a prosperous desirable colony and the pattern and viability of her worker brood is normal, she is an obvious choice for breeding. It may be that the bees in the colony will make preparations for superseding her. You can safely use any spare supersedure queen cells with advantage.

QUEEN INTRODUCTION

The basic principles governing the successful introduction of queen cells, virgin queens and mated laying queens to a broodnest in a bee colony are summed up in a twofold statement:

The broodnest must be compatible with what is to be introduced and 'like' replaces 'like'.

In queen-rearing the use of selected queen cells to replace other queen cells or to be placed in nuclei which have no

Photograph 8 Replacing the comb with the queen cell. Note the use of covercloths and the comb gap in the broodnest.

Photograph 9 The queen cell accepted and the young queen about to emerge.

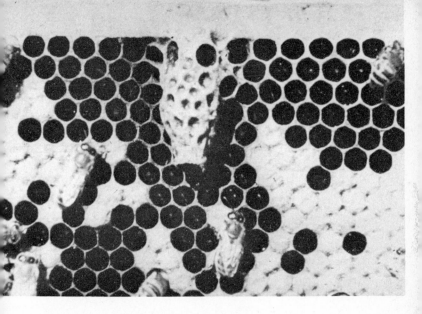

Photograph 10 The queen cell recently vacated.

Photograph 11 A comb of brood of a young mated queen.

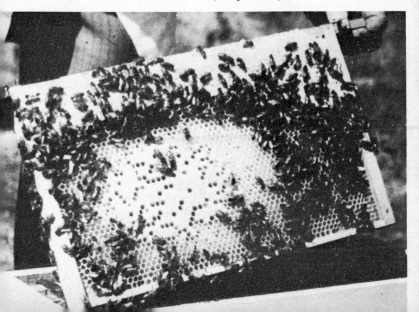

means of making a replacement queen illustrates these principles. To try to impose a queen cell on the bees in a broodnest where there were eggs and young brood would be against the natural instinctive behaviour of the bees. A mated laying queen could, however, be introduced because this type of broodnest would be compatible with the presence of a laying queen.

A virgin queen is more difficult to introduce except on those occasions when the condition of the broodnest is conducive to her acceptance. Her compatible broodnest would be one which had no eggs or open brood and from which ripe queen cells had been recently removed. Another compatible condition would be a nucleus colony with only broodless, queenless but well-fed bees or where the introduced virgin would replace another virgin.

A mated laying queen is the easiest to introduce since she might well be found in almost any type of broodnest — except one which had *laying workers*.

If a colony has been without a queen for some time then laying workers can appear. Lack of queen substance to inhibit the abortive development of the ovaries in a few of the workers means that they can sometimes lay a few unfertilized drone-producing eggs. Several of these eggs may be deposited in a single cell. Most of the eggs are not viable; those that do develop are in scattered patches of dwarf dome-shaped drone cells.

Some strains of bees produce laying workers sooner than others. Their appearance depends to some extent on the condition of the broodnest. Where this still contains open worker brood or queen cells the chances of laying workers appearing is much less. If a good nectar flow is occurring this also delays their appearance.

To deal with this problem of laying workers in a broodnest, the first step is to give the bees a chance of survival by putting in a comb of eggs and young brood. This young brood will need the brood food or bee milk of the nurse bees; the laying workers deprived of this special food will cease being able to produce eggs and useless queen cells will be made on the comb of young brood that was put in. A substitute ripe selected queen cell might then be accepted or a queen introduced. It is usually a better plan to unite the broodnest and bees, after destruction of any queen cells and drone cells, to a queen-right colony — providing it was worth the trouble. Unless it was very strong in bees it is seldom worth while. Instead make increase and replace it.

Another important factor in introducing queens to the bees in a queenless colony is the timing of the introduction and the attitude or behaviour of the queen when introduced. This is overcome by introducing the queen in a cage from which the bees in the colony can free her in a day or two. A very useful and convenient cage is the one Dr Butler and Mr Simpson used when carrying out extensive research, at Rothamsted, into the reliability of the introduction of virgin and mated laying queens directly or in a simple wire-mesh cage. (*Bee World Reprint* E 14.)

This simple cage is easily made of $\frac{1}{8}$ in. wire mesh — not perforated zinc — and is about 3 or 4 in. long x $\frac{1}{2}$ in. x $\frac{3}{4}$ in. One end is plugged with wood and the other end, after the queen alone has been placed in the cage, is covered with a single thickness of newspaper secured firmly with a tight rubber band. With a minimum of disturbance this caged queen is placed in between two combs in the broodnest of the queenless compatible colony. Hungry, she solicits food from the bees who can only contact her through the $\frac{1}{8}$ in. wire mesh. While feeding her the bees are able to obtain queen substance from her. She is soon released by bees who chew through the newspaper and accept her into the colony.

The introduction of a laying queen alone in this type of cage has a very high degree of success.

Some beekeepers may purchase queens. These will arrive by post in a wood and wire travelling- or postal cage, which is furnished with candy and has some worker bees in with the queen. Full instructions are printed on a card secured to the wooden back of the cage. If the instructions are properly carried out and the piece of card covering the candy exit/entrance hole is removed, there is a good chance that the introduction will succeed. If the accompanying workers are removed and the queen is alone in the cage her acceptance is enhanced.

Laying queens should not be kept without food for more than half an hour. Travelled queens will not have been in lay for some days. I would always prefer to introduce such a queen, alone in a wire-mesh cage, in the late evening to a well-fed three-comb nucleus of good-tempered bees. Later when the queen is laying unite the whole nucleus to the queenless colony by the newspaper method described at the end of this chapter.

Another simple and very reliable form of introduction — chosen from over thirty different methods — involves using a well-aired matchbox and tepid water. 'Well-aired' means that the matchbox should not be smelling of brimstone from the recently removed matches. The laying queen is put in the matchbox alone and taken to the colony which had been dequeened some two to six hours previously. The matchbox with the queen in it is then half filled with lukewarm or tepid water and the queen 'washed' for a few seconds before the water and queen are emptied into the broodnest. Provided there is no excluder under it this can very conveniently be done through the central feed-hole in the coverboard and so will involve no disturbance of the bees. The bedraggled queen is quickly cleaned and fed by the bees and in so doing they lick off her secretion of queen substance and her acceptance is quickly established.

When virgin queens have to be introduced to a compatible broodnest — in practical beekeeping this is very seldom — the simple cage or matchbox method can be used with success.

All introductions and uniting should be done with the minimum use of smoke and as little disturbance as possible.

UNITING
In practical beekeeping the uniting of two colonies of bees is often necessary. One colony should always be made queenless before uniting is done. It is too much of a risk to let

Diagram 9

UNITING

EXC = EXCLUDER
NP = SHEET OF NEWSPAPER

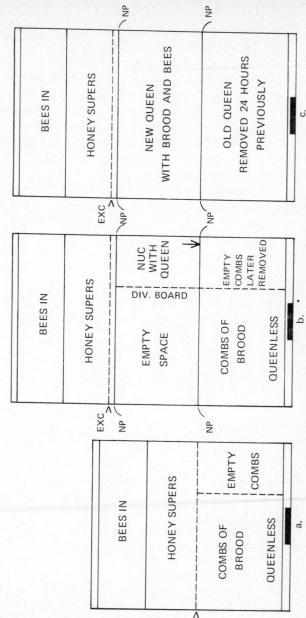

For the uniting, situation (a) is changed to situation (b).

the queens fight it out, for the victor herself may be damaged and in the spring the colony will be queenless.

Both colonies should be in broodchambers and before the uniting is done they should be moved close together. It is generally best to leave the queenless unit on its own site, especially if it still has honey supers on it. Over this queenless broodnest place a full single sheet of newspaper in which some holes have been made with a matchstick or pencil point. At dusk, the queen-right colony is placed on top of the newspaper. Another sheet of newspaper and an excluder should now be placed over the top of this broodchamber containing the queen before replacing any supers. The queen-right colony is thus sandwiched between the two sheets of newspaper. The two lots of bees unite peaceably after having chewed their way through the paper. Little pieces of paper outside the entrance shows when this has happened. Do not disturb the arrangement for a week or so. After that time the colony can be reduced to a single broodchamber if required and the empty combs taken away. (See Diagram 9.)

CHAPTER 8
Honey Production

Everything that we do with the colonies in the apiary has or should have a bearing on honey production. All systems of management should aim at increasing the average yield of surplus honey from all the overwintered colonies.

The maximum yield of honey is obtained from the strong, well-balanced, well-housed, healthy colony of a good strain of honeybees, headed by a young prolific queen, working with an uninterrupted rhythm in good weather in an environment of nectar-producing flowers.

This kind of colony is also the one that would require the least management — and one every beekeeper would like to possess.

The methods and manipulations described in spring and summer management, swarm control and queen-rearing, are directed to establishing this type of colony in the apiary. For honey production the essentials of good management should secure and keep the maximum force of bees of foraging age with replacement young bees and sealed brood in the colony during the whole of the main nectar flow. The colony should be sited as near as possible to the source of nectar.

The beekeeper, according to his skill, is able to achieve these conditions in many, if not all, of his colonies. By moving his bees to out-apiaries he can place them in a good nectar-producing environment.

Nectar production in flowers is dependent on the type and strain of plant and the condition, composition and aspect of the soil in which it is growing. Not every acre of white clover in full bloom has the same potential for producing nectar.

There is always another controlling factor — weather conditions. Records of the honey production of bee colonies in past years show a direct correlation between high yields of honey and good summer weather. In Britain, this is particularly the case since there are so many areas with very different micro-climates. It is these that influence honey

89

production in different localities. In many other countries good summers everywhere are almost a certainty.

In addition to the good management of his colonies the beekeeper must seek out the good districts in which to place them and then hope for good weather during the nectar flow.

Extracted Honey. Bees naturally store surplus honey above and at the sides of the broodnest. The addition of boxes of combs above the broodnest as extensions for honey storage saves the bees from making comb or extending the broodnest downwards as they would do when in an unconfined space. The excluder prevents the queen from laying in combs that will later be extracted for honey.

Clearing Bees from Honey Supers. When the nectar flow is over leave the honey storage supers on the colony for one or two weeks so that the honey can be fully ripened. Then, usually in mid-August in Britain, these supers can be cleared of bees and taken indoors in order to extract the honey.

A clearer board, fitted with at least two bee escapes, is put under one, or at the most, two honey supers. The bees can go down but not come up through the one-way bee escapes, and after about thirty-six hours most, if not all, of the bees will have been cleared from the combs in the honey supers.

The clearing of bees from supers in this way, though usually quite effective, involves two operations. Many different methods of speeding up the clearance in one operation have been tried. The combs of sealed honey can be taken out, one by one, and the bees shaken off on a board in front of the hive. After shaking, the beeless combs are put in a spare box and kept covered until taken away. This method has the disadvantage that when unripe honey comes out of shaken combs it can be the cause of robbing.

Alternatively, a bee repellant can be used. Of these repellants, benzaldehyde or artificial oil of almonds as used in other foodstuffs is the one recommended. It is the same chemical that I advised for use when making a subduing-cloth, but made stronger and more efficient by sprinkling about one small tablespoonful of benzaldehyde evenly over an 18 in. square cloth, or sheeting. This cloth *must* be kept in

90

a tightly covered jar since the vapour quickly evaporates in the open air. To use it, first give a puff of smoke at the hive entrance to subdue the guard bees, take off the roof and loosen the top honey super from the one below. Then remove the crownboard (chapter 4 — basic routine 16) and shake the bees from it. Puff some smoke across the tops of the exposed frames of sealed honey in this top super and wait about half a minute. Then quickly put the strong subduing-cloth over the honey super and immediately cover it with the crownboard. Leave it on for about twenty to thirty seconds. The warmer the weather, the less is the time needed. Take off the crownboard, put the cloth back in the jar and put on the screw cap. Remove the honey super after checking that it is free of bees and put the crownboard back on top of the second super. Keep the removed super of honeycombs covered with an ordinary covercloth and after restoring the roof on the hive take the super away out of reach of any bees.

Proceed to the next hive and, using a similar routine, take off the top super. The cloth will usually remain effective for clearing five or six supers, one at a time, provided the benzaldehyde is not allowed to evaporate in the open air. Six supers of honey are quite enough for one full evening's extraction of the honey.

When dealing with a super left next to the excluder over the broodnest, one precaution should be taken. First place an empty super on the excluder and put the remaining honey super on top of it before carrying out the clearing operation. This is necessary in order to prevent the repelled bees from struggling through the excluder and into the broodnest, which would become so overcrowded that the bees might even be forced out at the entrance. The depth of action of the repellant vapour of benzaldehyde is about seven or eight inches. This is why only one super is effectively cleared at each operation.

I have found this method of clearing bees from supers both rapid and efficient in operation. The vapour does not taint the honey neither does it harm the bees.

Uncapping and Extracting Honey.　　Not so long ago

before extractors became available the honeycombs, after uncapping, were cut out of the frames and put in a large strong porous cotton bag. Then in a warm kitchen this bag was hung up over a bowl and squeezed. The honey ran out and dripped down into the bowl. This was a simple country method and involved little or no expense. The wax combs were; however, destroyed.

Today the honey extractor is in general use. One holding six shallow combs or three deep combs is a convenient size for beekeepers whose total honey production in a good season may be four or five hundredweights. If possible, the extractor should be firmly fixed to the floor, or better still to a well-made, stout wooden framework or bench, high enough for a 56 lb. honey tank and strainer to be placed under the tap in the base of the extractor.

Uncapping involves the removal of the wax cappings on the cells in the honeycombs in thin slices. Plan this operation and carry it out with care. Put some newspaper under the honey supers and elsewhere where honey may drip. Take out a comb of honey, remove the metal ends (if used) and with an old knife clean the outsides of the top, side and bottom bars. This is best done on more sheets of newspaper. Work on a bench or table with an easily cleaned top. Rest the comb on a pad of newspaper on the table and hold the comb firmly by the other lug and side bar so that the thumb and fingers are well out of the way of the uncapping-knife. Lean the comb a little towards the knife, so that, as you cut off the cappings from the bottom, the cut-off slices will not immediately stick on the honey of the cut surface. What is to be done with the slices of cappings? If not more than three supers of combs are to be uncapped then a very simple arrangement is to use a 12 in. or 14 in. wire flour sieve placed in a large round bowl. The slices of cappings will probably stick to the knife, and can be scraped off against the wooden rim of the sieve; any honey in them will drain into the bowl. When uncapping have a deep jug of very hot water near by to put the knife in. The knife is then wiped dry on a dishcloth before being used to take off more thin slices of cappings. A bread-knife can be used quite well but there are many specially designed uncapping-knives and uncapping-trays available from bee-appliance dealers.

Uncapped, the comb of honey is put in the cage of the extractor. The bottom bar of the comb should lead in the direction in which the cage rotates. When the six combs are in place, the handle is turned and the cage rotates, flinging the honey out of the cells, by centrifugal force, against the side walls of the extractor. Do the turning quite slowly at first and when the one side is partly extracted reverse the combs. Turn again and extract all the honey from the second side, reverse the combs again and finish off the first side. Why is this necessary? If the first side were too rapidly extracted, the weight of the honey in the other side, under the effect of centrifugal force, would cause the combs to break — especially if they were newly made from wax foundation.

Take out the extracted combs, put on new metal ends and replace the combs in the super. It is easier to put on new metal ends and later at leisure clean the old propolised ones by boiling them in an old tin with bleaching powder in the water. When clean and dry smear them with Vaseline and keep them for use later.

Straining and Bottling Honey. Proceed with the uncapping and extracting, and when the bottom of the extractor has two or three inches depth of honey, put a honey tank and strainer under the tap and let the honey fill the strainer. The strainer will have one or more fine mesh sieves in it; it also has a flange at the base. Additional straining is sometimes needed and is obtained by fastening some finely meshed material (stocking top, folded butter muslin or nylon organza) over the underside of the flange. This is to strain pollen grains and tiny pieces of wax from the extracted honey. When using the honey taps always be most careful about closing them because honey flows silently.

When it is full keep the honey tank in a warm place overnight. This will allow the air bubbles to rise to the top. Next day the honey can be bottled. Use the British Standard type of honey jar — clean and warm. Test by weighing how full the jar must be in order to have a net weight of one pound of honey. Metrication will shortly have to be taken into account, and conversion tables will be available for bee-keepers. The B.S. jar is, however, likely to continue in use for some time.

If possible, store the bottled honey in the dark in an even temperature. If there is a lot of honey it can be stored in large honey tins. Later these can be warmed and when the honey is liquid more bottles can be filled. If you re-use bottles, make certain that new waxed inner wads are put in the screw caps.

If you intend selling any bottled honey to the public, make sure that you comply with the special regulations governing the sale of honey as a foodstuff, as issued by the Board of Trade. The honey must be correctly labelled and must have been produced, processed and bottled under the hygienic conditions stated in the regulations.

To return to the sieve, now full of cappings with the honey dripping into the bowl. If this is kept overnight in a warm place with newspaper under it, almost all the honey will have drained into the bowl. This honey is put through the strainer. The wax cappings should be well washed in rainwater and allowed to dry. They can be kept in a plastic bag for use in a solar wax extractor or for melting down into cakes.

Cleaning Extracted Honeycombs. After the extraction of the honey has finished the beekeeper will be left with a stack of supers containing honey-wet combs. These can be given back to the colonies of bees to be cleaned up. If the supers have been numbered they can go back to the same colonies.

Each colony will have been left with a clearer board or a crownboard on top of the excluder over the broodnest. In the late evening go to the colonies, take off a roof, remove the bee escapes or other covering from the holes in the board and put the supers on top. Cover these supers with another board (hole closed) and put back the roof. Endeavour to complete this operation in all the colonies in the apiary at the same time in order to prevent robbing from breaking out.

The bees come up through the holes in the board and take
94 down and store all the honey in the broodnest below, leaving

the combs clean and dry. Unless further autumn feeding has to be done, these supers can be left as they are in the care of the bee colony until they are required for use next spring. This method, as well as saving trouble in wrapping and storing the supers elsewhere, keeps the combs in good condition and free from the ravages of the smaller wax moth.

It is not so satisfactory when supers are placed back on the excluder and not over a board because the bees will then often collect the honey and reseal it in little patches instead of taking it down into the broodnest.

Wax Extraction. One way of doing this is to use a large clean tin which will fit into a saucepan. The tin is one third filled with rainwater and put in a large saucepan in which water is kept simmering. The previously washed cappings are added to the tin. The hot rainwater melts the cappings and the molten liquid wax forms a layer on top of the water. Any dross in the wax sinks to the bottom of the tin. Stir the contents in the tin with a thin piece of stick when all the wax is melted. Take out the tin and put it to cool slowly. When cold the top cake of wax, which shrinks a little when cooling, can be removed, the tin cleaned and the operation repeated. Bee-appliance manufacturers will take these clean cakes of wax in part-exchange for new sheets of wax foundation. Specially designed wax extractors and clarifiers can be bought if a large amount of wax has to be rendered down into clean wax cakes.

Another method of rendering clean wax is to use a solar wax extractor. This apparatus is made by constructing a shallow tin-lined tray about 20 in. x 16 in. x 4 in. or larger and fitting double glazing on top of it. It should be propped up at an angle of about twenty degrees facing south. When available, wax cappings, pieces of bracecomb and old broken combs are put at the top of the sloping tray. The sun melts the wax which runs down to a fine wire sieve screen secured across the tray some five or six inches from the end. The dross is left behind. Some rainwater can be put in this bottom end and the melted wax will float on top of it. It can be constructed so that the wax runs into a separate tin.

This method is efficient — if there is enough warm sun. The wax produced in a solar wax extractor is usually of good quality and colour, since the sun's rays have a bleaching effect on it.

Producing Comb Honey. Some indication of this method of honey production was illustrated in Diagram 8a. The method of obtaining comb honey in the small 4¼ in. square section boxes requires considerable skill, the right type of bee, a populous colony and a good nectar flow in favourable weather.

If combs of honey or some sections are only required for home use, then it is best to put a few frames fitted with thin unwired foundation in a super. There are also special hanging frames which hold three of the small section boxes, each fitted with thin foundation. These hanging frames can be placed in between two evenly drawn-out combs of sealed honey in the supers. When full they are removed, any bees are brushed off and the full sections are taken out of the frames.

When a whole crate or rack — a specially made super-box to hold rows of sections separated by tin dividers — is used, then the bees have to be induced to use the sections. The rack of sections can be 'baited' with several partly drawn-out sections, perhaps with some honey in them. These bait sections can be obtained from hanging frames or carefully kept from the previous season. Usually one super of shallow drawn-out combs is put over the excluder in spring and when it is half full, at the start of a main clover flow, a rack of sections is placed below the super so that the bees must go through the small beeways in the sections. If there is a shallow extension of the standard broodchamber in the broodnest it is best to leave it on so that pollen is not taken into the sections.

To produce some overcrowding, the broodnest is often restricted to one standard broodchamber at the start of a nectar flow. This overcrowding will also make the bees go into sections, but only after filling up the flank combs of the broodnest with honey. A young queen in full lay helps to keep the broodnest from becoming a storage chamber.

96

This overcrowding is often responsible for the start of swarming preparations. When working for section honey any of the methods of swarm control described earlier should result in the foraging force of bees and its reinforcements remaining on the original site.

A large swarm, hived on to drawn-out combs, not foundation, will often work sections if a good nectar flow is in progress and the weather is favourable.

For some beekeepers the fact that when producing section honey or 'cut-comb' honey there is no need for uncapping, buying or using an extractor or bottling, comb-honey production is all important.

When working for heather honey the use of sections or shallow super combs fitted with thin unwired foundation is almost a necessity. Heather honey cannot be readily extracted in an ordinary extractor. A honeypress has to be used to squeeze out the heather honey from combs cut out of their frames, because it does not run out of the cells like clover honey.

In many cases beekeepers cut out the shallow sealed comb of heather honey and divide it into three portions. Each portion is wrapped carefully in thin cellophane, put in an attractive cardboard box with a cellophane window and sold by weight as comb honey.

Cut-comb Honey. Plastic containers (4¼" x 3¼" x 1¾" deep) each with a 'snap-on' transparent lid are available. A well filled and sealed shallow comb of honey can be cut into six suitable portions each about half a pound in weight. Thin unwired wax foundation should be used. (See p. 44 and diagram 6.)

Chunk Honey is obtained by cutting a similar comb into conveniently sized pieces or chunks. One chunk is put in a pound honey jar and extracted honey of the same kind is used to fill up the jar.

In all forms of honey production it is well to remember the old adage 'Cleanliness is next to godliness', and that honey is essentially a pure and valuable energy-making food.

CHAPTER 9
Preparation of Honey and Wax for Exhibition

Beekeepers have an excellent opportunity for advertising their produce at the various honey shows held in districts throughout Britain. Most county and many local Beekeeping Associations (see Appendix) hold Annual Honey Shows.

The show schedule usually lists separate classes for comb honey in sections and frames and for light, medium, dark, granulated and heather honey. At the larger shows there are additional classes for wax and sometimes for mead and displays of bee produce.

The preparation of an entry of two jars in any of the honey classes involves time and the entry must reach a high standard to gain a prize. Success or even commendation is not easily won.

Marketed honey should always be of a good quality and flavour, clean and attractively labelled. Honey shows are valuable in demonstrating to beekeepers what 'quality' honey should be like and to consumers what they should expect to receive when buying honey.

Extracted Honey. The grading of extracted honey into three shades of colour, though arbitrary, is a well-established practice. Standardized grading-glasses are put beside a jar of honey held against the light to show to which class the sample belongs. Light honey is the most popular class in honey shows and the best liked by most consumers.

At honey shows all the extracted honey, light, medium and dark, is judged on a comparative basis. The first check is to see that the entry is in its correct colour class. Then one class at a time is judged by carrying out a series of eliminating checks and tests. These inspections and tests are for cleanliness, brilliance, clarity, aroma, density, viscosity, colour (within the class) and flavour. All other factors being equal the flavour is usually the deciding one and, of course, this depends on the judge's palate.

The following might be a description of a winner in the

'light' class: 'Absolutely clean and free from any air bubbles, dust or scum on the surface or in the honey, clean cap and wad (both sides), brilliant and not in the least cloudy, of good aroma (clover, lime and so on), thicker in consistency and lighter in colour than most of the other entries, having a very pleasant taste'. The twin jar must be the same.

In his management of the colonies the beekeeper will have used new foundation in new or very clean frames and will have put these in supers, close-spaced so that the combs will be drawn out evenly and fully filled by very strong colonies.

After clearing and before any extraction, he should hold these new combs up to the light to see that only one colour of honey, the lighter the better, is in the comb and that it contains no stored pollen. The best of these combs — each *fully* sealed right out to the frame edges, and very evenly capped with white or pale cappings, and with good thickness and weight — he will carefully set aside as exhibition comb. After careful cleaning the comb is put in a glass-framed case with a removable top and is ready for entry in its class. The others he will carefully uncap, extract first when the extractor is clean and store, after straining, in a clean honey tin. This tin of honey is kept — with a very clean cloth, a linen handkerchief possibly, over the open top — in an airing-cupboard, to make certain that no moisture from the air is absorbed by the hygroscopic honey. No dust must get into the honey. Later this honey is again carefully strained through several layers of selected material and put into carefully chosen honey jars that have no blemish in the glass. These jars are filled a little more than is needed. They are covered with a clean cap and wad, lightly screwed on, and are again kept in a warm, dry atmosphere. Before entering them in the honey show the beekeeper will use a warm spoon to clear any dust or small bubbles on the surface and to reduce the honey to its correct level — never underweight and never too full. The honey is then kept cool. When staging his entry, he should polish the jars with a clean cloth and put a fresh polished cap with a new wad on each. Overheating, which often happens when honey is put in a warm oven to try and make it very thick, destroys aroma and can usually be detected by a judge.

Medium or dark honey is subjected to the same in-spections and tests as were used for light honey. These honeys are usually blends from different nectar sources. The flavours in medium and dark honey vary considerably and this factor becomes more important in the final selection.

Pressed heather honey usually has a class to itself. This honey will often show trapped air bubbles which will not be regarded as a blemish, but heather blends may be excluded if the schedule had stated 'heather honey'.

Granulated Honey. This honey should be light in colour and show no frosting. It should have a fine white grain throughout and when tasted should be smooth and not gritty. It must have a pleasant aroma and flavour and should not simply be sugary. The beekeeper exhibiting granulated honey usually reserves show-quality jars, or a tin, of his light honey. This honey may not be quite so thick as that shown. The honey can be stirred with a knitting-needle without making any air bubbles until it looks dull and cloudy. This is the beginning of granulation. If the beekeeper has a very finely grained sample of granulated honey he can add a teaspoonful of this to each jar as a starter before stirring it. The resultant granulation of the honey in the jar will follow the pattern of the fine crystals in the starter. Complete granulation may take only days, or some months, according to the kind of honey and how it is kept. To encourage quick and fine granulation, first remove any bubbles that may appear on the surface after stirring, put on the screw caps and then stand the bottles in the daylight of a north-facing window. Turn them half round each day. When the honey has set and is firm on top it is ready for showing.

Frosting is not an indication of poor honey. It is the physical result of uneven granulation in the dextrose sugar in the honey. The frosting is caused by the contraction or shrinking of the granulated honey away from the glass of the jar. Frosting is hastened by any rapid change in the temp-erature in which the honey is stored.

Section Honey. With sections, as with the comb for extracting, all the cells on both sides should be sealed and the comb fully built out to the sides of the section with no 'pop' holes. The capped surface should be even and the cappings should show no signs of any honey seeping through them. The honey in the sections should be of one colour. Such sections are again produced by a strong colony during a main nectar flow. When sections are being selected from a full rack some may be good and only faulted by a few unsealed cells of honey. If these sections are put in hanging frames, as explained earlier, in one super and the side combs in the super are of fully sealed honey, the empty cells in the sections will be filled in a day or two, provided that the flow is still on. Any other storage-honey supers on the colony can be temporarily removed to make certain the bees concentrate on the unsealed cells. The wood of sections should be scraped clean and free of propolis stains. The straight edge of a piece of glass makes a good scraper. If the outsides of the sections when made up are rubbed with candlewax, this will make staining less probable and more easily removed. Then each section for exhibition is put in a glazed box which will allow the judge to examine both sides of the two sections entered.

Wax for Exhibition. In a honey show the scheduled class for a cake of beeswax will stipulate that it should be a certain weight, usually eight ounces. The finished entry must be very close to the prescribed weight or it will be eliminated. The cleanliness, appearance, colour, aroma and texture of the wax and particularly the perfection of its moulding are the criteria on which judgment is based. The colour of the wax may range from a clear, even pale primrose to a deep buttercup according to the source of collected nectar. Streaky colour, specks of foreign matter, a wavy surface and a dull muddy colour are adequate reasons for rejection when the waxcake is judged.

To make an acceptable cake of wax, first select the best wax cappings. These will be the lightest in colour. When obtainable, cappings from heather honey are usually excellent. After a thorough washing in several changes of rainwater, spread the cappings on a sheet to dry in sun and air. Then carefully pick out any dark pieces of wax. If you have a solar wax extractor, clean it thoroughly and let the selected wax cappings be melted in the sun. When a solar wax extractor is used the washing of the cappings is not so necessary. In order to make an eight-ounce cake of wax you will need nearly a pound of clean wax at the start.

Choose a suitable mould; a *flawless* Pyrex dish of the right size usually proves suitable — it is plain inside and heavy and thick in section. Polish the inside thoroughly and then smear it round with an *odourless* detergent and dry it with a very clean cloth. Wax readily picks up odours from the air so be very careful at all stages. The oven, when used, should not remind you of a previous well-seasoned roast.

Make ready two clean earthenware jars — two-pound jam jars will do. One is placed in an oven at a *low* temperature to warm it and a small wire strainer with handle and with a piece of clean old flannel inside it is also kept warm. Filter papers can be used instead of flannel.

The mould is placed in a bowl on top of some thin flat pieces of wood of the same thickness. The other jar is placed in a saucepan three-quarters filled with water. This is brought nearly to the boil and kept simmering. Some of the clean selected wax is put in the jar and slowly melted. The rest of the wax is added until all is melted. When the wax is liquid, hot and clear, the other jar is taken from the oven and the molten wax strained through the flannel or filter paper into it. Do not use the last few ounces of wax which may contain some dross. Put this jar of strained wax back into the warm oven.

The bowl with the Pyrex mould should be placed on a perfectly level firm table. The mould should be checked, using a spirit level, to see that it is level in all directions. The bowl is now filled with very hot water until the water level reaches the height that the wax will be when it is poured into the mould. See that no splashes of water go into the mould. When the mould has become very warm, the jar containing the filtered or strained wax is taken from the oven and the wax is carefully poured into the mould until it reaches the required depth for an eight-ounce cake.

Very carefully put two pieces of wood across the bowl but not over the mould and cover the bowl with two or more non-fluffy towels. The pieces of wood prevent the towels from sagging into the wax. Do not jar the bowl or table at any time.

Night — when any interruptions are less likely to occur and doors are not opened to make draughts or slammed to cause vibrations — is the best time for this important final moulding. Leave the wax in the mould overnight. This not only removes any temptation to look at the wax too soon, it also ensures complete slow cooling. In the morning the wax will have cooled and set. Add to the water already in the bowl some more water of the same temperature until the water level completely covers the mould. Leave it to cool thoroughly and the wax cake will usually come freely out of the mould and float to the surface. If it sticks, a gentle tap on the base and side of the mould will free it. Be very careful not to damage the thin brittle edges of the cake of wax. Examine it, if it has any flaws or cracks, ponder and decide what has caused them. If faulty, the cake must be broken up into small pieces and the whole process of melting, straining and moulding must be repeated. This is sometimes necessary when a prize cake of wax has been broken or badly handled at a honey show or damaged during transit to or from a show.

If without blemish, the wax cake is carefully polished with a piece of silk and kept in tissue paper in a box. When exhibited it should be put in a glazed showcase, preferably one lined with black velvet to set it off. The wax cake when in the showcase should be in the same position as it was moulded, with its upper surface on view.

CHAPTER 10
Autumn and Winter Management

Autumn is another critical period in the seasonal life of a bee colony when the timely help of the beekeeper is needed. After the surplus honey — and it should only be a true surplus to the needs of the colony — has been removed, each colony should be prepared for wintering.

In August wasps become a nuisance and a threat to bee colonies, especially the smaller nuclei. The wasp is an expert robber and with its unbarbed sting can inflict death on many guard bees. This is the time to restrict the entrances of hives to a few inches so that they are more easily guarded. Destroy any wasp nests you can find in the neighbourhood. Do this in the late evening in the dark when wasps have finished flying.

At the end of August or in early September, arrange to do any uniting or requeening that is still needed. In early September each colony should be inspected to see that it has a mated laying queen not over two years old, that it has brood, and that it has sufficient stores of honey and pollen to last through the winter and next spring.

Spring feeding is best done in the autumn. This statement simply means that any emergency feeding needed in the spring is only a result of inadequate feeding — or of leaving an insufficient supply of the bees' own hard-won honey — in the colony in early autumn.

Each colony needs between thirty and forty pounds of stores. Records of weekly weighings of colonies show that from October to February only a little over half a pound a week is needed to sustain a normal colony in an average winter. When brood-rearing starts in March or earlier, the consumption rises rapidly. A comb full of stores is needed to produce a comb of brood, apart from what is needed by the bees to raise the temperature of the broodnest.

When assessing the stores in the broodnest make a record of the amount of stores in each comb. A full standard brood-comb sealed on both sides will contain about four pounds.

Thirty pounds of stores need eight such combs. It is seldom that a broodnest will contain this amount unless it is one that has returned from the heather. This is where the shallow super used as an extension of the broodnest becomes so valuable. It can provide the extra storage space. This extension, without an excluder under it, makes the broodnest large enough to hold all the stores needed and yet leave some empty combs in which the bees can cluster during the winter. The stores are in the natural position, above and at the sides of the broodnest, and the beeway between the two boxes enables the cluster to move more easily as the stores near it are used up.

It has been shown how important it was to encourage brood-rearing in May; it is equally important that there should be some brood-rearing in every colony in late August and early September. Three to five combs with good patches of brood at this time is what is needed. Old worn-out summer bees have little of their life span left and die during winter and particularly during the first flights in spring, but young bees, from brood hatching out in August and September, remain physiologically young bees and in spring begin their duties with a full life span ahead. As I mentioned earlier, summer bees may only live for five or six weeks; autumn-born bees live six months. Truly, a worker bee is as old as its glands.

Young queens in the colonies will usually lay eggs and so provide young bees in August and September. Feeding with sugar syrup raises the temperature in the broodnest and encourages breeding. In some strains of bee, particularly some Italian strains, the prolificacy of the queen is such that brood-rearing in August goes on apace and all winter stores are used up. This strain of bee does not suit most areas in Britain.

If, after inspection, the amount of stores for winter is thought insufficient, then feeding is necessary. Sugar syrup, made up in the proportions of 2 lb. of sugar to 1 pint of water, should be rapidly fed. In most apiaries, large tin feeders with holes in the recessed flanged lid are best for rapid sugar-syrup feeding. Feeding should be done in early September and

105

completed well before the end of that month in order to give the bees sufficient time to 'invert' the sugar in the syrup and store it (see page 10).

Remove any stored and cleaned supers, put the filled feeder over the feed-hole in the board on top of the broodnest and surround the feeder with an empty broodchamber. The supers are put back on top. Feeding completed, the empty broodchamber can be removed and the feed-hole left open to give through ventilation.

At the end of September, or very early in October, when the wasp troubles are over, remove the entrance blocks or slides and replace them with mouse guards secured across the whole entrance. The best mouse guards are those made from strips of metal with $\frac{3}{8}$ in. holes. This material is obtainable from most ironmongers.

Each colony should now be able to winter well and come out strong in bees in the spring. It will have a good queen, plenty of young bees, good combs in which to cluster and ample stores — and a dry home.

Ventilation should be provided by removing any covering over the feed-hole in the top crownboard and by giving a gap of $\frac{1}{8}$ in. between this top board and the super or brood-chamber it covers. Do this by freeing it and putting some matchsticks, or sliding in some nails ($\frac{1}{8}$ in. thick), to stop the coverboard from being stuck to the top edges of the box it covers. This will allow any moist, warm air rising from the bee cluster to escape. There is no need for packing above the coverboard. Bees need to be kept cool and quiescent in winter. Make certain that the roof is weatherproof and that the whole hive is a dry home for the bee colony.

What other form of productive livestock will look after itself for six months and allow its keeper time for other things, with no regular feeding, cleaning out or coddling to do?

It is hard for some beekeepers to realize that bees in winter do not need human comforts. Frost and cold do them no harm. Plenty of good food, good combs and a dry hive is all they need, and remember the best packing for bees — is bees, and not mothy discarded human clothing.

Throughout winter an occasional check of the hives in the apiary is advisable, particularly after gales and very heavy storms. If deep snow occurs there is no need to worry, the colony will not suffocate, but see if the hive is still dry when the snow melts. If snow is cleared away it cannot soak into the wood. The real danger with snow is that warm, bright, winter sun may encourage bees to make cleansing flights and get chilled or lost through lack of familiar orientation marks. In such conditions of sun and snow put a board or large slate to slope from above the entrance to the ground. This darkens the entrance and when the snow clears the bees can still use the entrance and go out at the sides of the slate or board.

Winter is a good time to move any colonies to a new position in the apiary, if this is necessary. The moving must be done without disturbing the cluster of bees. When the moving is done in December and January, in cold weather, there is no fear of many, if any, bees returning to the old site.

Soft *white* candy can be given to colonies whose food supply has been neglected — which should never happen. Candy is at best an emergency ration and does not compare with honey or stored sugar syrup as a winter food.

Bees in Winter. Honeybees are able to survive our winter conditions because they are cold-blooded creatures and have evolved the ability to cluster.

Mammals — this term includes human beings — are warm-blooded and have to maintain a constant body temperature whatever the environment by consuming heat-producing foods. The body temperature of the cold-blooded honeybees can fluctuate between 50° F (10° C) in winter to 90° F (32° C) in summer when they are engaged in brood-rearing. By close clustering on the combs in winter the loss of heat is minimized. By expansion and contraction the cluster acts as a kind of thermostat controlling the temperature within itself.

Although essential work with the bees has finished, the winter period provides the beekeeper with time and opportunity to clean and renovate spare equipment, make new equipment and browse over his records. This is the time for making plans for next season and for assessing how and why some manipulation went wrong and another proved its value. Above all, there are always bee books to read and new knowledge of the wonders of bee life to acquire. The greater the understanding of bees, the more is the pleasure to be found in beekeeping as a hobby.

In natural conditions few truly wild bee colonies suffer from disease simply because the rigorous conditions of life in the wild do not allow any weakened livestock to survive. The serious diseases of bees are fortunately few and can be classified into diseases affecting the brood and diseases (or infestations) of the adult bee. The latter, when diagnosed, can be treated and cured — if the treatment is early enough and the correct treatment is applied — by the beekeeper himself.

BROOD DISEASES

Two of the diseases of the brood are called *American Foul Brood* and *European Foul Brood*. These are serious diseases and are subject to the provisions of the Foul Brood Disease of Bees Order made by the Ministry of Agriculture, Fisheries and Food. This order empowers the Ministry to arrange for apiary inspections for the purpose of preventing the spread of foul brood and to require the destruction of affected colonies and the disinfection of hives and appliances, if after laboratory examination of a sample comb the presence of American or European Foul Brood is confirmed.

Most beekeepers join a local Beekeepers' Association and become subscribers to Bee Diseases Insurance Ltd. This is an insurance scheme designed to compensate subscribers, pro rata to their subscription, for losses incurred through the destruction of bees and combs as a result of foul brood. This insurance company is a specialist body of the British Beekeepers' Association.

In the counties of England and Wales there are appointed Foul Brood Officers. These officers, usually experienced beekeepers, are skilled in the diagnosis of foul brood and should be contacted if and when a beekeeper has very good reason to need a second opinion. The foul brood officer will examine the colonies and if he considers that it is a case of foul brood

109

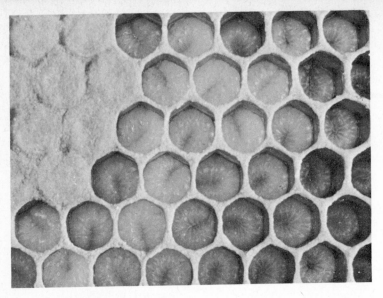

Photograph 12 Healthy brood.

Photograph 13 American Foul Brood: portion of comb showing four sealed cells (marked x) with cappings becoming dark and sunken.

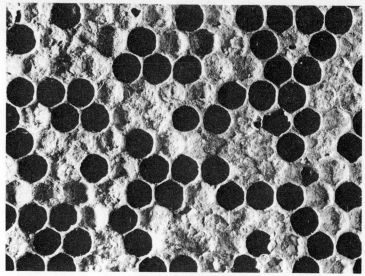

Photograph 14 American Foul Brood: open cells with cappings removed by bees and containing scales (not visible here).

he will take a sample broodcomb and send it for laboratory examination and tests to the Bee Advisory Officer, M.A.F.F., Rothamsted Lodge, Hatching Green, Harpenden, Herts., or to Trawscoed, Aberystwyth. He will then give the beekeeper an official 'stand-still' order so that if foul breed is finally confirmed by the Ministry tests any further spread of the disease is prevented.

Fortunately these diseases are seldom met with by most beekeepers. This does not lessen the need for vigilance and when examining a broodcomb during an inspection every good beekeeper will check it visually for normality in appearance and look closely at anything abnormal. Photographs 12 to 18 show normal healthy brood and combs affected by brood diseases. Within the scope of this book it is not possible to describe the causes, symptoms, appearance and treatment of these brood diseases. Beekeepers are recommended to obtain the bulletin *Diseases of Bees* or the advisory leaflets *Foul Brood* and *Minor Brood Diseases* (see Appendix).

Addled Brood is not strictly a disease since it is due to

some defect in the egg which is not revealed until the larva dies soon after it has been sealed. Here it is the queen who is the cause of the trouble and the cure is to requeen the colony — not from the same strain, but with a queen that produces normal brood. Addled brood is a relatively common occurrence and because it affects sealed brood and makes the cell capping moist and sunken, it may at first sight be mistaken for American Foul Brood. In addled brood the cell contents are *never ropy* and the body of the dead larva retains

Photograph 15 American Foul Brood: the 'ropiness' test.

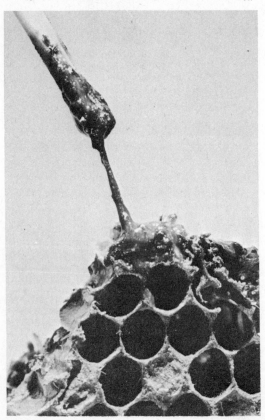

Photograph 16 European Foul Brood: note the unsealed larvae in various stages of collapse.

its shape for some days unless removed by the bees. Addled brood is not infectious and therefore combs need not be destroyed nor equipment disinfected.

Chalk Brood is usually associated with damp combs in damp hives. The cause of the disease is a fungus, *ascophaena apis* formely called *pericystis* which thrives in damp combs and on the contents of the bodies of some larvae. It is contagious. The dead larvae look like chalky white mummies loose in the cells. The badly affected combs should be burnt and the colony, if strong enough to be worth saving, should be transferred to a dry hive and good clean combs and later requeened. The old hive should be scraped and thoroughly disinfected and dried before re-use. Chalk brood must not be confused with combs containing mouldy pollen.

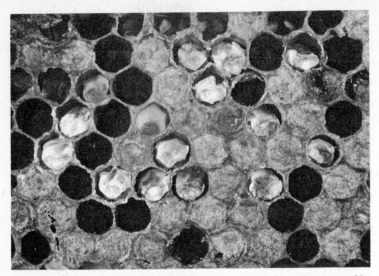

Photograph 17 Chalk Brood: white 'mummies' in cells uncapped by bees.

Photograph 18 Bald Brood: bald brood due to the presence of wax-moth larvae.

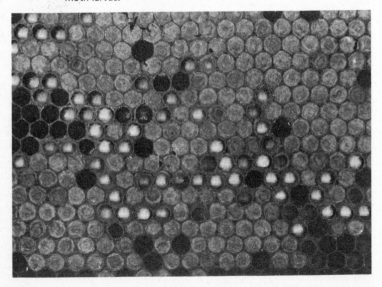

ABNORMAL BROOD

There are several conditions where brood is abnormal but not diseased.

Chilled Brood is usually caused by carelessness or inexperience. A nucleus colony may be given more young brood than the limited number of bees can properly care for. Brood, without sufficient bees to raise the necessary heat for its proper incubation, becomes chilled and dies. A dead larva may be black if young and greyish when older. Sealed chilled brood may show moist, sunken and perforated cappings but again, unlike American Foul Brood, the cell contents are never ropy.

Bald Brood is generally due to the ravages of wax-moth grubs that eat the cappings and the brood, which should be sealed, is exposed. The cells of bald brood are often seen in a small patch or line where a wax-moth grub has been at work.

Very occasionally a colony, free of any wax-moth grubs, will show pupae in uncapped or partially capped cells. Some of this brood may die, other brood may develop normally though unsealed. This type of bald brood is probably due to a genetic deficiency in the queen, and requeening with a mated and tested queen is the cure.

Patchy Brood. Quite often the sealed cells in a broodcomb will have a patchy appearance instead of being in an even regular pattern with no interspersed empty cells. These empty cells may be due to having had honey or pollen in them when the queen was laying eggs in the area; more probably they are due to some eggs not hatching out. An old, failing queen often lays some non-viable eggs.

Patchy drone brood can be produced by laying workers or by an unmated virgin queen, or an old queen who has become a drone-layer through lack of sperm in the spermatheca or a blockage in the sperm duct.

ADULT BEE DISEASES

Two diseases or infestations can affect adult honeybees and cause their death before they have spent many days in flying on foraging duties. In *Acarine infestation* small mites enter and breed in the thoracic breathing tubes (trachea). After hatching out the mites leave the tubes and migrate to infest other very young bees. Badly infested bees lacking the ability to fly can usually be seen crawling about in front of the diseased hive.

In *Nosema,* protozoon parasites affect the mid-gut of the honeybee and so weaken it that it expires when making its first flights in spring. A similar and often associated parasite, *Amoeba,* affects the Malpighian tubules (the kidneys) of the bee in like manner.

Where there is evidence of dysentery on the combs in the broodnest, samples of adult bees should be taken and sent for expert diagnosis. For detailed information of treatment the beekeeper is again recommended to consult *Diseases of Bees,* or the advisory leaflets *Acarine Disease* and *Nosema and Amoeba Disease* (see Appendix).

Dysentery. Bees normally void excreta on the wing away from the hive. Involuntary discharge inside the hive may be due to nosema or amoeba disease as described above. It is also, in the absence of these diseases, caused when bees have been confined in the hive for a long period during winter with no opportunity of making a cleansing flight. Continual jarring of the hive, as in transportation, can also cause dysentery. Where no disease is diagnosed, remove fouled combs as soon as possible, replace them with clean combs and give the bees a feed of thick warm sugar syrup.

Bee Paralysis is a general term covering many illnesses of bees caused by poisonous nectar or pollen (rhododendron, laurel, foxglove and so on). Adult bees may have shiny, greasy-looking bodies and seem to tremble. They are often attacked by other bees. Usually the symptoms disappear, but if persistent, requeening should be tried. If a great proportion of the bees are affected, then the colony is best destroyed. Such serious cases of paralysis are uncommon.

Spray Poisoning occurs when bees have been gathering nectar or pollen from a source that has been sprayed with a substance that is toxic to bees. In serious cases there is a sudden reduction in the number of foragers and clusters of dying or dead bees may be inside the hive or near the entrance. If possible, collect a sample of two hundred bees and send these to the Bee Advisory Officer at the Rothamsted address given earlier in this chapter. Make inquiries concerning any spraying that has occurred in the area and send full details of the occurrence with the sample of bees. Move the hive away to another site.

TAKING A SAMPLE OF BEES

When a diagnosis of the health of adult bees is needed, a sample of about thirty bees will be required by the County Bee Advisory Officer, or the Officer at Rothamsted or Trawscoed, Aberystwyth. To take a sample some empty matchboxes and a thin, stiff piece of celluloid or plastic about 4 in. x 2 in. are needed. When the bees are flying well make the entrance as small as possible and then, when a lot of returning bees are trying to enter, place the inside of a matchbox over them. Slip the piece of celluloid underneath the box and look through it to see how many bees you have trapped. Slide the matchbox cover on as you slide off the transparent celluloid. If you have not trapped sufficient bees, repeat the operation with another matchbox. The same technique is used to gather bees from a comb. In this case make certain the queen is not trapped. With skill and some practising on drones, individual bees can be picked up and put in a matchbox.

Label each box with a hive identification number, secure the box with a tight elastic band or Sellotape and enclose a letter giving your name and address and a request for diagnosis. Four matchboxes go inside a foolscap envelope at ordinary postal rate. See that the envelope flap is well stuck down. On the back of the envelope write 'Bees for examination'.

STRAY SWARMS

Beekeepers often acquire stray swarms, either because they have been asked to 'take' them from a near-by garden or because an unknown swarm has taken possession of an empty hive in the apiary. A stray swarm is not necessarily a free gift. A wise beekeeper will always subject such a swarm to a period of quarantine. Hive it in a single broodchamber on one clean drawn-out comb and three or four frames of foundation according to the size of the swarm. Place it on a site well away from other colonies. Take a sample of bees from the swarm in a matchbox and send them to the Bee Advisory Officer for examination for Acarine and Nosema diseases. Do not feed the swarm for three or four days. During this time it will use up any infected honey the bees may have been carrying in their honeysacs. Then feed the swarm with about four pints of sugar syrup. In three weeks the sealed brood can be checked for any brood disease and the swarm can be declared healthy, or be destroyed.

In conclusion, make sure you purchase bees from a source which will give a guarantee of the health of the bees supplied. If you start with healthy bees there is little to fear from disease. Ample stores of honey and pollen in good clean sterile combs in a weatherproof hive, coupled with a plan of breeding from the best queen in the apiary, help in keeping the colonies strong and healthy at all times. A good beekeeper is never just a keeper of bees.

APPENDIX

Beekeeping Associations

BRITISH ASSOCIATIONS

Since each county in Great Britain has several local units, it is not possible here to give a complete list of addresses. For an address of a County Beekeepers' Association write to:

The General Secretary, British Beekeepers' Association, 55 Chipstead Lane, Riverhead, Sevenoaks, Kent.

For an address of a County Beekeeping Instructor write to:
The Beekeeping Advisory Officer, Ministry of Agriculture, Fisheries and Food, Rothamsted Lodge, Hatching Green, Harpenden, Herts.

OVERSEAS ASSOCIATIONS

For an address of a Commonwealth or Foreign Beekeeping Association or Advisory Department write to: .

The Editor, *Bee World,* Hill House, Chalfont St Peter, Gerrards Cross, Buckinghamshire, England.

Further Reading

British Beekeepers' Association *Bee Craft* (monthly)

Bee Research Association *Bee World* (quarterly); *Reprints from Bee World*

Bent, E.R. *Swarm Control Survey*

British Bee Journal (fortnightly)

Butler, C.G. *The Honeybee; The World of the Honeybee*

Dade, H.A. *Anatomy and Dissection of the Honeybee; Laboratory Diagnosis of Honeybee Diseases*

Fraser, H.M. *History of Beekeeping in Britain; Beekeeping in Antiquity*

Hamilton, W. *The Art of Beekeeping*

Hodges, D. *The Pollen Loads of the Honeybee*

Ministry of Agriculture, Fisheries and Food — Bulletin No. 9 *Beekeeping;* Bulletin No. 100 *Diseases of Bees;* Bulletin No. 134 *Honey from Hive to Market;* Bulletin No. 144 *Beehives;* Bulletin No. 206 *Swarming of Bees;* Advisory Leaflets: *Acarine Disease* (A.L. 330) *Beeswax from the Apiary* (A.L. 347); *British National Hive* (A.L. 367); *Examination of Bees for Acarine Disease* (A.L. 362); *Feeding Bees* (A.L. 412); *Foul Brood* (A.L. 306); *Importance of Bees in Orchards* (A.L. 328); *W.B.C. Hive* (A.L. 411); *Migratory Beekeeping* (A.L. 344); *Modified Commercial Hive* (A.L. 468); *Nosema and Amoeba Disease* (A.L. 473); *Minor Brood Diseases* (A.L. 561)

Ribbands, R. *The Behaviour and Social Life of Honeybees*

Snelgrove, L.E. *Swarming; Queen Rearing; Queen Introduction*

Wadey, H.J. *The Behaviour of Bees; The Bee Craftsman*

INDEX

121